The Tweed

D1329332

pocket mountains ltd

Published by
Pocket Mountains Ltd
Holm Street, Moffat, DG10 9EB
pocketmountains.com

ISBN: 978-1-907025-37-2

Introduction

Rivers have been at the centre of Scottish life for thousands of years. For the earliest settlers a river meant survival – a source of food, drinking water and transport. Over the centuries villages, towns and all of Scotland's cities have grown and developed along the banks of a river.

From the Industrial Revolution, when Scotland was one of the manufacturing powerhouses of Europe, until the long decline of heavy industry in the 20th century, rivers were integral to Scotland's economic development.

As towns and cities attempt to reinvent themselves in the wake of that decline, rivers and riverbanks are crucial to regeneration, providing key destinations for residential developments, offices, leisure and recreation. Water activities such as rowing, sailing, kayaking, canyoning and fishing are increasingly popular, and wildlife is making a comeback as the environment begins to recover from pollution.

From source to sea, a river passes through a variety of landscapes – from mountains to hills, towns to cities, countryside to concrete – and the best way to discover the scenery, wildlife, architecture and history is to walk.

The increasing number of paths and walkways along riverbanks present plenty of opportunities to explore. Whatever your ability – walking at high or low level, following tough terrain or a simple route – this series offers something for everyone.

The River Tweed

At 96 miles in length the River Tweed is the fourth longest river in Scotland, although for the last few miles of its journey it crosses the border into England. The close proximity of the countries has bestowed an intriguing history upon the River Tweed. It has been a boundary for thousands of years, and was a crossing point both for trade between Scotland and England and for marauding armies. A number of bridges span the River Tweed and have played key roles in the story of this beautiful river.

The Scottish Borders have, at times, been unfairly judged as a poor relation of the Scottish Highlands. However, the sense of tranquillity the landscape engenders, the wildlife and the scenery soon dispel that notion. The term 'lowlands' is a misnomer, as the Border country has an abundance of higher ground, granting some superb walking opportunities.

The 25 routes in this guidebook have been chosen to illustrate the varied landscapes, and thus the diversity of walking, to be found on and near the banks of the River Tweed as it travels from source to sea. Many of these routes are circular to take in the best of the scenery in the area around each stage of the river's journey and to explore some of the most interesting towns and villages that

have grown up along its banks. The walks also highlight the wildlife, architecture and history to be found along the way.

A place apart

In common with the land north of the Highland Boundary Fault, the Scottish Borders has its own dialect. The language of the Scottish Borders is distinct from much of Scotland and derives from the 1st Millennium when the region was a Celtic culture. An early form of Welsh was spoken, which can still be detected in names such as Kelso, Peebles and Galashiels.

By the Middle Ages, English had become the dominant language: Broughton, Selkirk, Berwick and the many Laws (Dollar Law, Kirkhope Law and Broomy Law, for example) that rise above the River Tweed have their origins in Old English. The derivation of the name Tweed is vague, but possibly stems from the Brythonic *tau* or *teu*, which mean 'strong', 'silent' or 'flowing'.

The source of the River Tweed is Tweed's Well, found in rugged moorland approximately six miles north of Moffat. It is a lonely setting, and a number of little burns trickle down from the surrounding hills to join the burgeoning Tweed as it travels north and then east.

Several significant rivers, such as the Teviot, Ettrick, Yarrow and Lyne, flow into the River Tweed as it meanders through the Scottish Borders, running along the

The Tweed at Hay Lodge Park, Peebles

Northumbrian Border and entering the North Sea at the magnificent walled town of Berwick-upon-Tweed. On its route, this great river runs through bustling, historic towns and villages such as Peebles, Melrose, Dryburgh, Gala and Kelso.

Over the course of its journey, the River Tweed runs beneath the higher ground of Annanhead Hill, Broughton Heights, Drumelzier Law, the stunning Glensax Horseshoe and the iconic Eildon Hills, all of which grant superb views.

It travels through some beautiful expanses of woodland and alongside great swathes of rich, fertile farmland. The riverbanks, woodland and farmland are alive with roe deer, otter, kestrel, heron, kingfisher, buttercup, red campion, bluebells and ramsons.

Early history

The very earliest Stone Age and Neolithic hunter-gatherers used the river as a means of transport, travelling in traditional boats such as the currach. The river was also a source of food and water. During the next few thousand years, as the land was farmed more intensively, cattle, sheep and pigs provided important sources of food, milk and clothing.

The Bronze Age and the Iron Age saw more definite roots being laid down, particularly by the Votadini tribe. Forts were built on Cademuir Hill near Peebles and the Eildon Hills above Melrose, the latter being home to a community of around 2000 people for many years.

The Romans, too, were attracted to the shapely outline of the Eildon Hills, and when Julius Agricola led his army across the border in 79AD they paused near Melrose at Newstead – reputedly the oldest inhabited village in Scotland – and stayed for the next 150 years. Trimontium, a fort, was built at the base of the Eildons and was at the height of the Roman occupation home to around 1500 soldiers.

The environs of the Tweed are also home to some of Scotland's most important and celebrated buildings. The illustrious abbeys of Melrose, Kelso and Dryburgh were built along the banks of the river during the 12th century. Great castles, such as Roxburgh, Norham and Berwick were primarily a form of defence, but also a focal point for the bustling towns and settlements that sprang up along its banks.

The close proximity to England was a double-edged sword – trade links were strong, but Edward I of England looked longingly at Scotland, and he invaded with devastating effect in 1296, leaving a litany of destruction in his wake.

Major battles like those at Flodden and Philiphaugh, near the River Tweed at Selkirk, as well as the activities of the Border Reivers in the 16th century, led to a succession of governments proclaiming that the Borders were becoming as problematic as the Highlands.

As the 18th century and the Industrial Revolution approached, the River Tweed was the source of a remarkable economic expansion along its banks. Although the Borders were far removed from the heavy industry of Central Scotland, the textile industry proved to be an unqualified success, employing thousands of people and putting many of the towns along or near to the Tweed, such as Peebles, Galashiels, Innerleithen and Selkirk, on the map.

The production of knitwear, cashmere, hosiery and linen flourished, as did tweed. It is wrongly assumed that the river gave the cloth its name – the original name, *tweel*, was the Scots name for twill, a type of weave. A merchant misread *tweel* as tweed, and subsequently it became known by this name. By 1821, Galashiels alone was home to ten mills. Mill owners prospered, but it was hard graft for the mill workers, who worked six days a week under tough conditions.

The economy in the Borders was also helped by the arrival of the railway. The Edinburgh to Carlisle line was constructed between 1847 and 1862, and generated jobs through the export of coal. However, during the 19th and 20th centuries, the majority of the stations and lines closed. Mass production of textiles meant that many of the mills could not cope with the workload, and today only a few exist, although the world-famous quality of the textiles has not diminished.

Over the centuries, writers and painters, including Sir Walter Scott, James Hogg and J M W Turner, have all depicted the River Tweed in a favourable light, drawing tourists into Scotland's southeast corner. Innovations in fly-fishing by the Victorians meant that great rivers, particularly the Tweed, became incredibly popular with anglers. Nowadays, the River Tweed has become one of Britain's great salmon and trout rivers, providing around 15 percent of all salmon caught in Scotland.

These days, manufacturing still accounts for 20 percent of local jobs but, like much of rural Scotland, the Scottish Borders has used the landscape to boost its economy and create work. Fishing still plays an integral role and outdoor tourism, focusing on activities such as cycling and walking, has made the region a major draw for outdoor enthusiasts.

How to use this guide

The walks in this guidebook run from the Moffat Hills above the source of the Tweed to the sea at Berwick-upon-Tweed. Wherever possible, the start/finish for each walk is easily accessible by public transport and, if not, there is car parking nearby. The majority of the walks are also easily reached from the villages and towns along the length of the River Tweed, with access to shops, places to eat, accommodation and public toilets.

Each route begins with an introduction detailing the terrain walked, the start/finish point (and relevant grid reference), the distance covered, average time to walk the route and the relevant Ordnance Survey (OS) map.

Public transport information is also detailed, although this may change from time to time and should be checked before commencing any of the walks in this guide (travelinescotland.com).

A sketch map shows the main topographical details of the area and the route. The map is intended only to give the reader an idea of the terrain, and should not be followed for navigation – the relevant OS map should always be used for this purpose.

Every route has an estimated round-trip time. This is for rough guidance only and should help in planning, especially when daylight hours are limited. In winter or after heavy rain, extra time should also be added for difficult conditions underfoot.

Risks and how to avoid them

Some of the routes in this guidebook are challenging hillwalks whilst others cover more remote terrain. The weather in Scotland can change suddenly, reducing visibility to only a few yards. Winter walking brings distinct challenges, particularly the limited daylight hours and the temperature – over higher ground, temperatures can fall well below freezing. Please take this into consideration before commencing any of the hillwalks in this guide. Preparation for these walks should begin well before you set out, and your choice of route should reflect your fitness, the conditions underfoot and the regional weather forecasts.

Even in summer, warm waterproof clothing is advisable, and comfortable, supportive footwear with good grips is a must. Don't underestimate how much food and water you need and remember to take any medication required, including reserves in case of illness or delay. Do not rely on receiving a mobile phone signal when out walking in the hills or remote areas. It is a good idea to leave a route description with a friend or relative in case of emergency.

There is a route for almost all levels of fitness in this guide, but it is important to know your limitations. Even for an experienced walker, cold, aches and pains can turn an easy walk into an ordeal.

Those routes that venture into the hills or rough terrain assume some knowledge of navigation with use of map and compass, though these skills are not difficult to learn. Use of Global Positioning System (GPS) is becoming more common; however, while GPS can help pinpoint your location on the map in zero visibility, it cannot tell you where to go next and, like a mobile phone, should not be relied upon.

Access

Until the Land Reform (Scotland) Act was introduced in 2003, the 'right to roam' in Scotland was a result of continued negotiations between government bodies, interest groups and landowners. In many respects, the Act simply reinforces the strong tradition of public access to the countryside of Scotland for recreational purposes. However, a key difference is that under the Act the right of access depends on whether it is exercised responsibly.

Landowners also have an obligation not to unreasonably prevent or deter those seeking access. The responsibilities of the public and land managers are set out in the Scottish Outdoor Access Code (outdooraccess-scotland.com).

The walks within this guidebook cross land that is only fully accessible due to the co-operation of landowners, local councils and residents. Some of the routes pass through farms, golf courses and streets, and near homes and gardens.

Cyclists and horse riders often use the paths and tracks, and anglers and canoeists may use the river and riverbank. Consideration for others should be taken into account at all times and the Scottish Outdoor Access Code must be followed.

At certain times of the year special restrictions are implemented at low level and on the hills, and should be respected. These often concern farming, shooting and forest activities: if you are in any doubt ask. Signs are usually posted at popular access points with details: there should be no presumption of a right of access to all places at all times.

The right of access does not extend to use of motor vehicles on private or estate roads.

Seasonal Restrictions

Red and Sika Deer Stalking:
Stags: 1 July to 20 October
Hinds: 21 October to 15 February
Deer may also be culled at other times for welfare reasons. The seasons for Fallow and Roe deer (less common) are also longer. Many estates provide advance notice of shoots on their websites.

Grouse Shooting:
12 August to 10 December

Forestry:
Felling: All Year
Planting: November to May

Heather Burning:
September to April

Lambing:
March to May − although dogs should be kept on leads at all times near livestock.

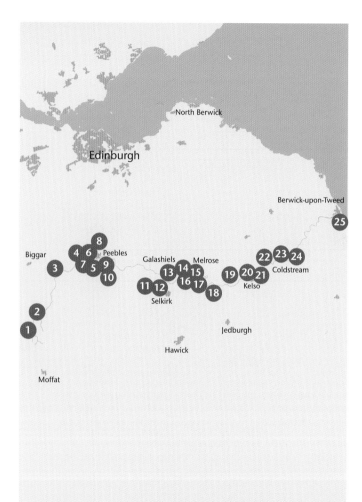

The Walks

The Devil's Beef Tub

Annanhead and The Devil's Beef Tub

Distance **8km/5 miles**
Time **3 hours**
Start/Finish **A701 lay-by, 6 miles north of Moffat GR NT056127**
Terrain **Hill, moorland paths and field paths, single-track road. The path around the Devil's Beef Tub is very exposed**
Map **OS Landranger 78**
Public transport **Regular Stagecoach Service X74 between Glasgow and Moffat, but this leaves around six miles to the start**

This walk over Annanhead Hill, just south of the source of the River Tweed, journeys around the Devil's Beef Tub, a remarkable place where the hillsides drop steeply into the glen below. The Strait Step section of the walk is perhaps not for the faint-hearted, and care should be taken, but easy tracks then head by Ericstane Farm and onto a section of the Annandale Way, leading back to the start via a short diversion to a Covenanter Monument.

► From the A701 lay-by go through a gate onto the Annandale Way, follow a broad track for a few metres, turn right over a wooden footbridge and pass through a gate. Turn left where a broad grassy path travels over a slightly wet area, but then quickly improves as it begins to climb steeply northeast alongside a fence and a conifer plantation. Pass a couple of marker posts to reach the trig point on the summit of Annanhead Hill; a great spot to look over the Moffat Hills and towards the source of the River Tweed.

► Continue east, with a drystone wall to the left, over Peat Knowe with the grassy slopes plummeting away on the right into the glen below. Continue to follow the path to the head of the Devil's Beef Tub beneath Great Hill.

Dancing with the Devil One of the most thrilling sites in this part of Scotland is the Devil's Beef Tub, a deep hollow formed by hills to the north of Moffat. It was once called the Corrie of Annan, but when members of the notorious Johnstone clan used it to hide stolen cattle it became known as the Beef Tub, or the Marquis of Annandale's Beef-stand. The Devil's Beef Tub is part of Corehead, which is famous for its association with William Wallace; his sister married Sir Thomas Halliday, the laird of long lost Corehead Tower. Wallace is reputed to have gathered men from Ettrick Forest and Border clans here to lead his first assault on the English at Stirling Bridge in 1297.

► From the gully turn right onto the Strait Step path which makes its way south around the edge of the ravine. Care must be taken here as the path runs very close to the edge – the walk at this point is nothing less than enthralling with great views down into the glen and back to Annanhead Hill. As the path descends into the glen it can become a little indistinct, so keep to a southerly bearing traversing the grassy slopes of Great Hill to reach a fence and a gate above a burn.

► Don't go through the gate; instead continue east along the grassy path, keeping the fence to the right. Follow this towards Corehead Plantation and a gate. Go through here and carry on to reach the wood; turn right, walk alongside the wood and then turn left around its edge to reach a gate beside the houses at Corehead.

....

Dragoon's Den A memorial commemorating John Hunter is on the southwest rim of the Beef Tub. Hunter was a Covenanter killed while fleeing from dragoons led by Colonel James Douglas in 1685. He had been hiding out in a house at Corehead and was attempting to escape by running up the side of the Beef Tub when he was shot. A stone just south of the Strait Step marks the spot where he died and he is buried a few miles away in Tweedsmuir.

► Go through the gate and continue by the old farm outbuildings to a footbridge. Turn right over the bridge, go through a gate, turn right and follow the field a few metres to another gate. Once through, turn left onto a single-track road signposted for Ericstane. Walk south along the road away from Corehead, passing through tranquil countryside, for approximately one mile to arrive at Ericstane Farm.

► As you come to Ericstane look for a rough track to your right (signposted 'Footpath') and follow this through a gate to climb steeply away from the farm. As height is gained further superb views open out, particularly towards the 808m-high Hart Fell. The walled track ascends through a gate, past a house and then through another gate. Beyond the next gate (again signposted 'Footpath') turn right onto another farm track, which maintains a gradual ascent until it passes through a gate to arrive at the A701.

► Carefully cross the road and then go through another gate onto the Annandale Way. Follow the waymarked track north as it climbs through a gate and over the moorland terrain of Ericstane Hill with the indistinct summit providing a fine view of Annanhead Hill. The track then drops down by waymarkers to return to the A701.

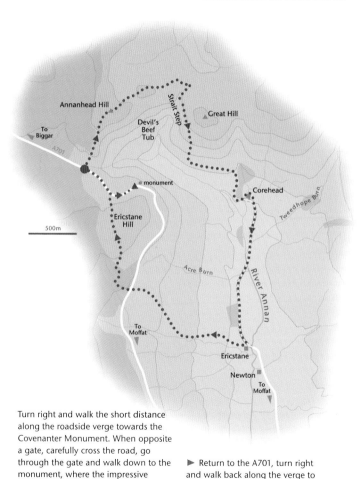

Turn right and walk the short distance along the roadside verge towards the Covenanter Monument. When opposite a gate, carefully cross the road, go through the gate and walk down to the monument, where the impressive Devil's Beef Tub awaits.

► Return to the A701, turn right and walk back along the verge to the start.

Covenanter Monument above the Devil's Beef Tub

Drumelzier and Pykestone Hill

Distance 14km/8.75 miles
Time 4 hours 30
Start/Finish Main Street, Drumelzier
GR NT135342
Terrain Hill paths, moorland, single-track road. One steep ascent and descent. Sections of pathless terrain
Map OS Landranger 72
Public transport First Scotland Service 62 between Edinburgh and Peebles. Scottish Borders Council Service 91 between Peebles and Drumelzier. There is limited parking in Drumelzier

The hills above Drumelzier provide a stimulating walk over the rounded summit of Pykestone Hill and the pronounced cone of Drumelzier Law. These sprawling hills give comprehensive views across much of Southern Scotland.

► From Drumelzier Main Street (B712) take the 'no through road' opposite a phonebox and walk by several cottages onto a farm track. Once by a farmhouse the track veers left onto a grassy track with the Drumelzier Burn to the left. Beyond two gates, it rises gradually to

a fork. Bear left, following a stony track through another gate where the route then crosses the Drumelzier Burn by a footbridge.

► Keep straight on as the now grassy track climbs southeast through a pocket of woodland to a fork. Go left, then at the next fork go right. Climb southeast along a narrow heather-bound path over Den Knowes to reach a Landrover track. Turn left and follow the track southeast onto Den Knowes Head where there are fine views along the Clyde Valley. The track then crosses a flatter section of ground, but as it swings south leave it and climb spongy, heathery slopes onto the 737m summit of Pykestone Hill, which is a fine vantage point to look across to the Culter Fells and Tinto.

► From the summit descend southwest, following a line of fenceposts onto a flatter, boggier portion of moorland to reach a junction of fenceposts on Long Grain Knowe. Turn right, keep the fence to your left and follow it northwest along a broad ridge towards Glenstivon Dod. Where the fence ends, an

Wizards and Castles According to legend, the wizard Merlin is buried near the village of Drumelzier; the spot is marked modestly by a thorn tree. Drumelzier Castle was the ancient seat of the Tweedie family, before being passed on to the Hay family in 1632. Today, its ruins lie within farm buildings, some of which were built using stone from the castle.

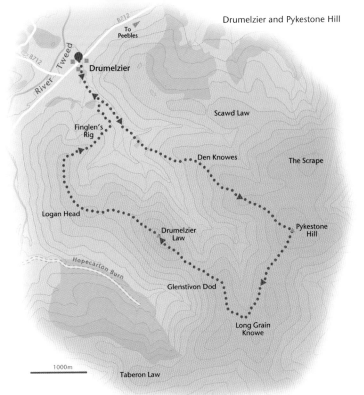

indistinct path is picked up. Follow this northwards to reach a large cairn on Glenstivon Dod. Here the path forks. Bear left for a section on which the path drops sharply northwest over heathery ground, passing another cairn. A very steep ascent leads onto the summit of Drumelzier Law, which is a good point to take a breather and enjoy the wonderful panorama.

▶ A short, steep descent reaches flatter ground with the path continuing north over Logan Head and then northeast down Finglen's Rig. The path peters out as it drops steeply over heather, then grassy ground to reach a fence. Cross the fence, turn left onto a grassy path and descend steeply by a wood to reach the outward track. Turn left and follow it back to Drumelzier.

Pykestone Hill

Green Law and Broughton Heights

Broughton Heights

Distance **11.5km/7.25 miles**
Time **5 hours**
Start/Finish **Main Street, Broughton**
GR NT113367
Terrain **Roadside verge, minor road,
hill paths and tracks. Some steep
ascents and descents**
Map **OS Landranger 72**
Public transport **First Scotland
Service 62 between Edinburgh and
Peebles. Scottish Borders Council
Service 91 between Peebles and
Broughton. There is a small car park
at Shepherd's Cottage after
Broughton Place Farm**

The author John Buchan spent
many of his summer holidays in
Broughton, and this hillwalk begins
from the village. Part of the walk is
on the excellent John Buchan Way,
which runs between Broughton and
Peebles, before leaving it to climb
over the lovely rolling hills of Green
Law, Broughton Heights, Hammer
Head and Trahenna. With good
paths and tracks these hills provide
a superb high-level tramp.

► Starting from the corner of Biggar
Road (B7016) and Main Street (A701),
walk north out of Broughton along the
roadside verge for 200m, and then turn
right from the A701 onto a single-track
road, signposted 'Stobo'. Follow this
road as it wends its way through
woodland to climb by Broughton
Place Farm. Continue into open
countryside to pass a small car park
and Shepherd's Cottage. Go through a
gate onto the waymarked John Buchan
Way (JBW). Walk straight on along a
grassy track, which rises steadily by a
pocket of woodland and then descend
gently to cross the Hollows Burn by a
wooden footbridge.

► The good broad path then
climbs steadily north through heather,
beneath the steep-sided incline of
Clover Law with the higher slopes of
Hammer Head in front. Follow this to a
fork beside a John Buchan Way marker
post at the base of Broomy Side.
Take the left branch where the path
continues its ascent to reach a second
JBW post. Turn right here and then bear
left, leaving the John Buchan Way
behind to climb the steep, heathery
slopes of Broomy Side.

► Further up a path is gained, which
is followed to a fence. Turning left,
continue to follow the path to another
fence near the summit of Broomy Side.
Cross this and then turn right onto an
obvious track, which rises gently (with
the fence to your right) north over
Broomy Side and then more steeply
onto Green Law where fine views of
Broughton Heights and Drumelzier
Law dominate.

23

► The track then dips gradually northwest, leading to one final climb north onto Broughton Heights (at 571m the highest point of the walk). This is a spacious vantage point to enjoy a fine panorama over the likes of Broad Law and Tinto. Retrace your steps to the junction of fences beneath Broomy Side. Cross the fence and descend steeply south on a narrow, heathery path to return to the JBW.

► Turn left through a gate and follow the path by two JBW marker posts to a fork. Bear right past a third marker post and then turn sharp right from the JBW onto an indistinct path which climbs onto a broader grassy track. Follow this track east along the lower slopes of Hammer Head to gain another track. Turn right onto a narrow path and from here it is a steep climb southwest onto Hammer Head. A broader track is eventually gained which continues to a fence. Cross this to reach the cairn on Hammer Head's summit.

► Cross back over the fence and then turn right onto a track. Follow the track and fence south and then southwest along firm moorland - this is a fantastic high-level walk along a broad upland table, with swift and skylark darting about in summer. The track eventually bears left away from the fence and climbs steadily southeast to reach another fence and a gate. Go through the gate and continue to the top of Trahenna Hill where great views along the River Tweed await.

► Descend from Trahenna and return through the gate beneath the summit. Climb between a wall and a fence (the ground is rougher underfoot) to a gate. Pass through the gate, turning left onto a track which drops steadily southwest onto a flatter plateau. Here, pick up an indistinct path on the right and follow this as it drops down the heathery hillside, broadening as it descends over grassy slopes to return again to the John Buchan Way. Turn left and retrace your steps to Broughton.

....

The Baron Hills John Buchan loved walking the hills and glens near Broughton when he holidayed at his grandparents' house in the late 19th century. The wonderful outlook from Green Law and Broughton Heights will have changed little in subsequent years, and the renowned author and 1st Baron Tweedsmuir would surely have revelled in the extensive views of the Pentland and Galloway Hills and, on a clear day, the Lake District mountains.

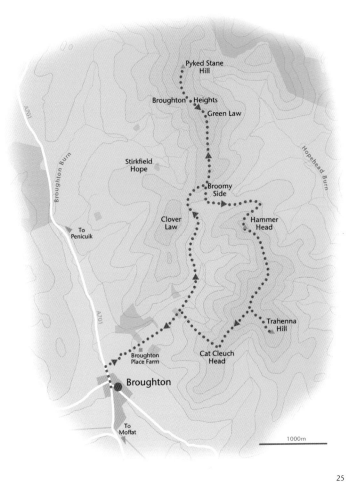

Pyked Stane Hill

Broughton Heights

Green Law

Hopehead Burn

Broughton Burn

Stirkfield Hope

Broomy Side

Clover Law

Hammer Head

A701

To Penicuik

Trahenna Hill

Broughton Place Farm

Cat Cleuch Head

Broughton

To Moffat

1000m

Broughton from Trahenna Hill

John Buchan Way at Harrowhope

The John Buchan Way

Distance **21km/13 miles**
Time **6 hours**
Start/Finish **The Old Free Kirk, Broughton GR NT114356/Bank House High Street, Peebles GR NT251404**
Terrain **Pavement, minor road, hill paths and tracks. Waymarked throughout. Some steep ascents and descents**
Maps **OS Landranger 72 and 73**
Public transport **First Scotland Service 62 between Edinburgh and Peebles. Scottish Borders Council Bus Service 91 between Peebles and Broughton**

The John Buchan Way between Broughton and Peebles travels through some of the Scottish Borders' remoter glens, as well as over higher ground with exceptional views. Although there are some fairly steep ascents the walking is generally easy going, and the clear waymarks and paths (some of which have been used by travellers for hundreds of years) make this route one of the finest along the River Tweed. The walk begins beside the Old Free Kirk in Broughton (which housed the John Buchan Museum until 2012) and finishes at the Bank House in Peebles, a former Buchan family home.

▶ From the Old Free Kirk walk north out of Broughton for 200m, turning right onto a single-track road signposted 'Stobo'. Walk along the road past a farm and Broughton Place, and continue into open countryside to pass by a small car park and Shepherd's Cottage. A grassy track leads by a small wood and then down over Hollows Burn via a footbridge. The path then climbs steadily through a peaceful glen, levelling out as it travels around the base of Clover Law, following waymarks, towards Broomy Side. A steeper climb up the lower slopes of Broomy Side reaches another waymark. Go right here and descend gently to a gate. Go through the gate and stick to the main track as it descends east by Hammer Head, through a wilder landscape with some fine views of Penvalla. The track eventually drops down to the lonely cottage of Stobo Hopehead.

▶ Bear right onto a track and follow this for approximately 500m to reach a waymark pointing left. Leave the track, descend a grassy path and cross a footbridge over the Hopehead Burn. A steeper path then contours southeast round the lower slopes of Penvalla (there are superb views here along the glen), with the gradient easing as a waymarked fork is attained at the top of the climb.

▶ Take the left branch and descend to another fork. Go right and continue to drop gradually southeast through the scenic glen of Harrow Hope. The path makes for easy walking and in due course crosses a stile and passes a lovely Scots pine wood. It then crosses the Easton Burn by a bridge beside the ruin of Harrowhope. The track sweeps right away from Harrowhope and continues alongside the Easton Burn through a mixture of woodland and farmland, crossing a couple of stiles, for 0.75 miles.

▶ Just before a bridge, the track splits into three. Bear left onto the middle track (signposted JBW) and continue over two more stiles to meet a single-track road. Turn right to follow the road down to the B712. Go right (signposted 'The Glack 2 miles') and walk along the verge for around 200m, passing Stobo Kirk, to reach a road opposite a cottage.

▶ Turn left here, cross a bridge over the Tweed and follow the rough road towards Easter Dawyck farm. Before

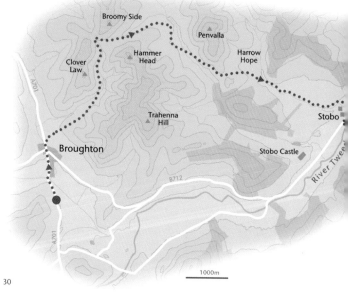

1000m

reaching the farm turn right over a stile (waymarked) into a field. Follow the waymarks around the field's right-hand edge, alongside a wall. Go through a gate, cross a farm track and turn right through a gate onto another farm track. At a fork bear right, go through a gate, then turn left onto a waymarked path. A footbridge crosses a burn to a grassy path which leads you steeply up open hillside, soon bearing left to climb gradually northeast around the shoulder of the hill.

► After a waymark the path runs alongside a wall, bearing left at a fork. Keep the wall to the left as you head across moorland and over a stile by a gate. Follow a field edge and waymarks downhill over a stile to cross another field on a muddy track. After another two stiles turn left onto a single-track

Buchan's Steps Known chiefly as a prolific author of both fiction and non-fiction, John Buchan was also the 1st Baron Tweedsmuir and served as Governor General of Canada from 1935 to 1940. Born in Perth in 1875, Buchan spent his formative years in Fife, studied in Glasgow and enjoyed many summer holidays in Broughton where his grandparents lived. He relished the wildlife and walking opportunities the local hills and glens presented. As an author Buchan is best known for his spy thriller *The Thirty-Nine Steps*, which was subsequently adapted as a film by Alfred Hitchcock in 1935. The Chambers Institution in Peebles, founded by publisher William Chambers, now houses the 'John Buchan Story' which celebrates his life and works.

road at The Glack. Follow this quiet road as it swings right (signposted 'Peebles') down to a road signposted 'Peebles via Cademuir'.

▶ Turn right to carry on over the Manor Water and around the base of the Cademuir hill forts for about one mile. After the second entrance for Cademuir Farm turn left onto a path, which continues alongside the road and then bears left onto a broader track. This rises steadily to reach a dip between the hill forts and Cademuir Hill.

▶ At a fork go left to a waymark. Carry straight on to another fork and bear right. Continue to follow the waymarks as the path traverses the lower slopes of Cademuir Hill with wonderful views of Broughton Heights and Peebles opening out. The path finally drops down to a gate beside some houses. Go through the gate to descend a broad grassy track to a final gate. Beyond this, turn left onto Edderstone Road and then right onto Craigerne Lane. Follow the waymarks into Peebles town centre at the B7062 (Kingsmeadow Road). Turn left and cross the Tweed Bridge to reach Bank House and the end of the walk.

Peebles from the John Buchan Way

Cademuir Hill

Distance **9.25km/5.75 miles**
Time **2 hours 30**
Start/Finish **Kingsmeadow car park, Peebles GR NT255401**
Terrain **Pavement, single-track road, hill paths and tracks. Some steep ascents and descents**
Map **OS Landranger 73**
Public transport **Regular First Scotland Service 62 between Edinburgh and Peebles**

Cademuir Hill is one of the smaller hills that surround Peebles, but is no less interesting than the town's loftier summits. Beginning by the banks of the River Tweed, the route follows part of the John Buchan Way (JBW) onto the wonderful vantage point of Cademuir hill forts. A minor road travels through beautiful countryside back to Peebles.

► Exit Kingsmeadow car park onto Kingsmeadow Road (B7062) and cross onto Caledonian Road. As the road sweeps right, go straight on to follow a lane which climbs to Chambers Terrace. Turn right and then left onto Frankscroft at a John Buchan Way sign. The pavement narrows to a paved path which continues by playing fields to Craigerne Lane. Cross here, turn right (again waymarked) and follow a path beside Craigerne Lane onto Edderston Road at a JBW sign.

► Turn left and follow the road a few metres to a gate on the right. Go through the gate and follow a grassy path by a cottage through another gate where it immediately forks. Go right to climb gradually up the hillside by the JBW – now a good grassy path – following this southwest onto the lower slopes of Cademuir Hill. Once over a crest, the path forks again. Take the left branch which gives views to Broughton Heights and Tinto.

► Continue to follow the waymarked path as it skirts Cademuir Plantation and over Cademuir Hill to reach steeper slopes beneath the fort. At this point ignore a John Buchan Way sign, which

Cademuir Community Several thousand years ago two forts sat on the summit ridge of Cademuir Hill and a substantial Iron Age community utilised its fine vantage point. The higher fort, which may have housed about 40 timber-framed buildings, was built when the lower fort became too small for the community. It is thought both forts were abandoned when the Romans advanced around 80AD. The view can be breathtaking, with Hundleshope Heights, Culter Fell and the Pentlands all on show. The River Tweed threads its way around the fringes of Cademuir's lower slopes.

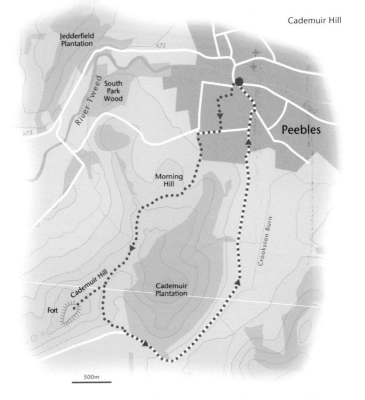

points left. Instead take the right path, which climbs steeply to reach the highest point (407m) of the fort.

▶ Retrace your steps down to reach the first John Buchan Way signpost passed on the way up. Turn right and descend a good path southeast beside a drystone dyke. As the wall turns sharply left leave the JBW and bear left onto a grassy path, which drops steeply to a track beside Cademuir Plantation. Turn right and walk a short distance to a single-track road. Go left to follow this quiet road through glorious countryside for two miles, heading back into Peebles onto Bonnington Road. Upon reaching Springwood Road turn right, then left onto Springhill Road and descend back to Kingsmeadow car park.

Broughton Heights from Cademuir Hill

Peebles and Neidpath Castle

Distance 5.5km/3.5 miles
Time 1 hour 30
Start/Finish Kingsmeadow car park
GR NT255401
Terrain Pavement, single-track road, riverside and woodland paths. One steep ascent
Map OS Landranger 73
Public transport Regular First Scotland Service 62 between Edinburgh and Peebles

Leaving from Peebles, the River Tweed is followed through Hay Lodge Park (named after the Hay family, Earls of Tweeddale) and around the base of the impressive 14th-century Neidpath Castle. Crossing the River Tweed at Manor Bridge, a steep climb up an old road leads to one of the finest viewpoints in the Scottish Borders – the outlook from here is ample reward for the effort required to reach it. A lovely woodland walk then drops back down into Hay Lodge Park for the return into Peebles.

► From Kingsmeadow car park, turn right onto the B7062, cross the Tweed Bridge and then turn left to descend a road past the swimming pool into Hay Lodge Park. Join the riverside path, turn right and make your way through the park, where there are lovely views along the River Tweed and of Peebles – here,

birds such as goldeneye, red-breasted merganser and goosander are seasonal visitors. Once across a footbridge over a burn, continue to a flight of steps.

► Climb these and then turn left through an opening in a wall. Follow a path down a flight of steps and continue through the park via a combination of paved paths and grassland. When you reach the western edge of Hay Lodge Park, bear left to leave it for a path signposted 'Neidpath Castle'. Cross a footbridge to follow a pleasant riverside path which makes its way through a lovely copse of Scots pine and over

A House for de Haya The four-storey towerhouse of Neidpath Castle was built around 1370. The Sheriff of Peebles, Sir William de Haya, built the original structure in the early 14th century, but much of what we see today dates from the 16th and 17th centuries. The castle was visited by Mary Queen of Scots in 1563 during one of her processions through Scotland. In 1650, its 12ft-thick walls managed to withstand an assault from Cromwell's troops for a time, although they succeeded in damaging much of the castle. The Hay family subsequently sold it to the Duke of Queensberry in 1686, and it was allowed to fall into disrepair. In 1810 the Earl of Wemyss inherited the castle, and it still belongs to the family today.

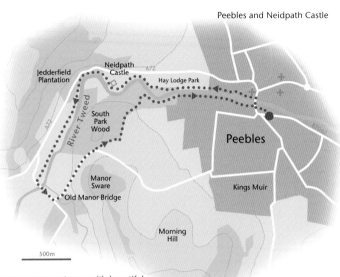

some craggy outcrops with beautiful views of the Tweed. Cross another footbridge and go through a gate to follow the path around the dramatic profile of Neidpath Castle perched on the crag above.

▶ The path now undulates through some craggy outcrops and down through another gate to continue beneath steep, wooded embankments. Carry on beyond the next gate to reach another of the great bridges that span the Tweed along this route – the splendid eight-arch viaduct of Neidpath Bridge (see Walk 7 for more information). Fork left underneath the bridge to take the path alongside the picturesque Tweed, eventually climbing a short, steep slope to a gate.

Go through here and turn left onto a dismantled railway, which provides an excellent means of travelling through the magnificent Borders landscape.

▶ Follow the track to reach the five-arch Manor Bridge. Go through a gate, turn left and follow the Kirkton Manor Road, branching left after 100m to descend a narrow road and cross the single-arch Old Manor Bridge where the road climbs steeply to reach a small car park and a viewpoint at Manor Sware. The view over the Manor Bridge and along the Tweed Valley to the distant hills are fantastic. Another car park a few hundred metres along the road provides an equally arresting view across Peebles and to the higher ground above the town.

▶ Continue past the car park and, after about 100m, turn left from the road to go through a gate signposted 'Peebles via South Park'. Follow a path into Manor Sware woodland to a fork. Take the left option, which continues straight on through the woodland. The path then drops gently to another fork where you go right for a meandering section down through predominantly birch/beech woodland to another fork. Again go right and follow the path to a fence, which accompanies it down a flight of steps, continuing above the River Tweed and back towards Peebles.

▶ The path then reaches the dismantled Peebles/Symington railway. Follow this easy, level path to a junction. Turn left and follow a track down to Hay Lodge Park at the River Tweed beside a footbridge. Don't cross the bridge; instead turn right and follow the paved riverside path through the park, eventually returning to the Tweed Bridge. Go up a flight of steps, cross the B7062 and descend another flight of steps back into Kingsmeadow car park.

Neidpath Castle

Tweed Valley from Manor Sware

Barns Tower

Peebles to Lyne

Distance **11.25km/7 miles**
Time **3 hours**
Start/Finish **Mercat Cross, Eastgate GR NT254404**
Terrain **Pavement, single-track road, woodland and riverbank tracks**
Map **OS Landranger 73**
Public transport **Regular First Scotland Service 62 between Edinburgh and Peebles**

The River Tweed has a number of beautiful bridges and several are visited when walking between Peebles and Lyne. An excellent riverside path leaves Peebles and passes the impressive remains of Neidpath Castle before continuing along the banks of the River Tweed, passing the Tweed, Neidpath and Manor Bridges. This part of the river is well known for its salmon and trout fishing, and you may see anglers casting their lines. A good part of the walk also utilises the old Peebles/Syminton railway line, which was closed in the 1950s.

▶ Facing the Mercat Cross at the corner of Northgate and Eastgate, walk west along High Street. Turn left at a roundabout, cross the B7062 and, just before the Tweed Bridge, descend right and follow a road by the swimming pool into Hay Lodge Park. Join the riverside path, turn right and follow the path

through the park, crossing a footbridge to continue to a flight of steps. Climb the steps, turn left through an opening in a wall and then drop down a flight of steps. Walk through the park via a combination of paved paths and grassland to reach a path signposted 'Neidpath Castle'.

▶ Bear left from Hay Lodge Park and cross a footbridge to follow a riverside path which climbs over some craggy

....

Bridging the Tweed The bridges between Peebles and Lyne are superb examples of design and engineering. The Tweed Bridge at Peebles dates from the 15th century. It was rebuilt in 1663 and further arches were added in 1799.

Further along the river is the impressive sight of the Neidpath Viaduct, sometimes known as the Queens' Bridge. This sandstone structure comprises eight archways and was built in 1863 by Robert Murray, a local architect, as part of the extension of the Symington to Broughton railway line to Peebles.

The five-arched Manor Bridge was built in 1883 whilst nearby, spanning the Manor Water, is the lovely little Old Manor Bridge, dating from 1702.

The Lyne Viaduct, opened in 1864, crosses the Lyne Water and was built as a result of the extension of the Symington railway line to Peebles.

outcrops and through a lovely stand of Scots pine. Cross another footbridge and go through a gate where the path continues by the imposing Neidpath Castle (see Walk 6 for more information), perched on the crag above. The path then undulates over more craggy outcrops. Carry on along the path underneath steep, wooded embankments to pass through another gate and then continue to reach a fork beside the skew-arch Neidpath Viaduct.

► Branch left underneath the bridge to follow the path along the River Tweed, eventually climbing a short, steep slope to a gate. Go through here, turning left onto a dismantled railway, which provides an excellent means of travelling

....

The Nobles of Barns The beautiful Georgian mansion of Barns House was designed by Michael Nasmyth in 1773. James Burnet of Barns, whose ancestors had settled here in the 1200s, commissioned the house. Prior to the building of Barns House, the Burnets had lived in the adjacent Barns Tower. It is thought to have been built in the late 16th century by William Burnet (4th Laird of Barns) and his wife Margaret Stewart – their initials W B and M S are carved above one of the upper floor windows. After 1773 the tower was probably used as servants' quarters, and today it is an unusual holiday let.

through the magnificent Borders landscape. Follow the track to reach Manor Bridge. Go through a gate, cross the road and then go up a flight of steps back onto the dismantled railway track. Walk along this peaceful track through beautiful countryside for around 1.5 miles to reach a bridge crossing the Lyne Water.

► Cross the bridge and then drop left down a single-track road to reach Lyne, which consists of a scattering of houses. The road makes its way through Lyne until it narrows down to a path and a footbridge over the Tweed. Cross the bridge and turn left into woodland, following a path by a cottage to reach the entrance drive to Barns.

▶ Continue straight on by Barns, turning left off the road at a sign for Tweed Walk after around 200m. Go over a stile into a field and follow a grassy path over two stiles to return to the River Tweed. Turn right and walk along the wooded riverbank path in the company of wagtail and common sandpiper, passing through a series of gates to return to Manor Bridge. Climb a flight of steps, go over a stile and turn right to follow a road. Turn left after 100m to descend a narrow road and cross the Old Manor Bridge where the road climbs steeply with spectacular views along the Tweed. Continue by a car park and Manor Sware woodland.

▶ The gradient eases as the road passes a second car park and then descends steeply by a farm, with further views over Peebles, to meet Edderston Road. Go left and follow Edderston Road back into Peebles, turning right to walk along Caledonian Road which ends at the B7062. Bear left, cross the Tweed Bridge and turn right into High Street to return to the start.

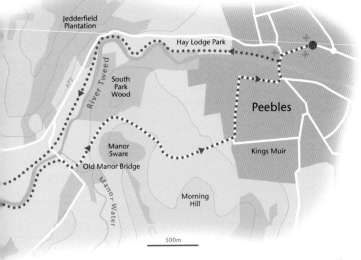

Hay Lodge Park

Peebles Hydro

Peebles and Soonhope Glen

Distance 5.5km/3.5 miles
Time 1 hour 30
Start/Finish Mercat Cross, Eastgate
GR NT254404
Terrain Pavement, single-track road,
woodland and glen tracks
Map OS Landranger 73
Public transport Regular First
Scotland Service 62 between
Edinburgh and Peebles

**Leaving from the lovely town of
Peebles, this gentle walk soon leads
to the quiet beauty of Soonhope
Glen. Excellent paths and tracks
throughout the route enable the
walker to focus on the stunning
views and abundant wildlife.**

► Facing the Mercat Cross on Eastgate,
turn left to walk along Eastgate, turning
left after Eastgate Theatre. Follow the
pavement through East Station car park
onto Edinburgh Road (A703). Cross
here, turn left, follow Edinburgh Road
for a short distance and then turn right
up a paved path to reach Venlaw
Quarry Road at the base of Venlaw
Community Woodland.

► Turn left, following the road to
Venlaw High Road. Turn right and climb
the road to a fork. Go left into Venlaw
Community Woodland and follow a
track with great views over Peebles. In
due course this sweeps left and

descends gently through the gate into
the open countryside of Soonhope Glen.
An excellent track progresses above
Soonhope Burn with some magnificent
views over Glentress Forest to Dunslair
Heights. The wildlife includes buzzard
and kestrel. The track undulates gently
for around half a mile to reach a path on
the right just before Glenbield Farm,
signposted 'Peebles and Glentress'.

► Descend this steep, grassy path
(taking care as it can be slippery) to
reach the Soonhope Burn, which is
crossed by a wooden bridge. Climb a
grassy path to a track, turning right onto
this to drop gently through beautiful
countryside. Once through a gate
continue by a little community of
distinctive huts, which were built by
miners from Rosewell during the 1930s.
Miners and their families, and then

Sheltered Housing Peebles' status as
an important agricultural area is
reflected in its Cumbric translation
Pebyll, meaning 'Place of Sheilings' –
sheilings were huts used by shepherds
for shelter during the summer months
when livestock grazed on higher ground.
The town has been a major trade route
between the Central Belt and the
Scottish Borders for centuries. Today
Peebles is a charming and lively town
with some of Britain's finest walking and
cycling right on its doorstep.

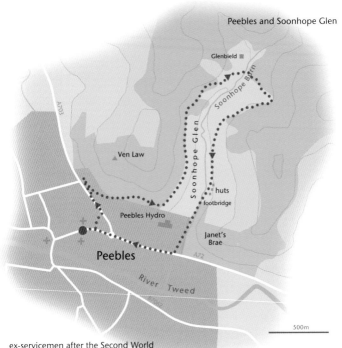

ex-servicemen after the Second World War, used the huts for leisure. Most are very idiosyncratic (one has been converted from a railway carriage) and sit in sharp contrast to the much grander Peebles Hydro, which stands nearby.

▶ The track eventually reaches the base of the glen and crosses back over the Soonhope Burn by a wooden bridge. Beyond Soonhope Farm and a gate, a minor road passes Peebles Hydro to arrive at Innerleithen Road (A72). Turn right and follow this road over Edinburgh Road and back to Eastgate.

Health Benefits The Peebles Hydro was opened by the Hydropathic Company in 1881, providing a variety of exotic-sounding remedies for guests. Set within 30 acres of the beautiful Tweed Valley, the original building was destroyed by fire in 1905, and it took another two years before the striking building we see today was opened. During the Second World War Peebles Hydro was used as a hospital for injured servicemen.

Soonhope Glen

Glensax

Glensax

Distance **19km/12 miles**
Time **7 hours**
Start/Finish **Glen Road, Peebles**
GR NT259392
Terrain **Woodland, hill and moorland paths and tracks, single-track road. Boggy terrain between Stake Law and Dun Rig. Some steep ascents and descents**
Map **OS Landranger 73**
Public transport **Regular First Scotland Service 62 between Edinburgh and Peebles leaves a walk of around a mile to the start**

At 742m Dun Rig is the highest point of the wonderful Glensax Horseshoe and also the highest hill in the Scottish Borders; it is a marvellous spot to survey the Borders landscape. Much of the route onto Dun Rig travels along an ancient drove road, and the walls enclosing the path are still in remarkable condition.

► From the end of Glen Road, walk by the entrance to Haystoun and go straight on into Gypsy Glen (signposted 'Gypsy Glen and the Old Drove Road'). Follow the woodland path southeast and, once through a gate, descend alongside the clear waters of Glensax Burn. A bridge then crosses the burn where the path climbs a flight of wooden steps. It continues to rise,

offering fine views over the Peebles countryside, eventually passing through a gate and out of the woodland. Here, a broad track ascends alongside well-maintained walls that enclose the route of the old drove road.

► Continue to follow the track southeast as it climbs steadily with views beginning to open out over Glensax to Newby Kipps, Preston Law and Cademuir Hill, as well as back over Peebles. Once through another gate, the track hugs the right-hand wall to reach a fork. The branch on the right takes a steeper, more direct line to a gate, but the left route follows the drove road for a more gradual climb alongside the left-hand wall with views along the Tweed, eventually returning to the right-hand track beside a gate. Go through this,

Driving Test From the 16th century, the route that climbed from Gypsy Glen and onto the hills on the eastern side of Glensax was part of the main drove road between the Highlands and the great trysts in England. Real skill was required to control and keep the livestock moving, and the drovers had to know the terrain intimately. Each drove could consist of between 400 and 1000 cattle walking 10 to 12 miles a day – upwards of 100,000 cattle were driven each year to the likes of Carlisle, Newcastle, Norfolk and London.

then head steeply southeast towards Kailzie Hill, with the views stretching all the way to the Pentland Hills on the outskirts of Edinburgh.

► The track then undulates its way over the almost imperceptible summit of Kailzie Hill where the right-hand wall ends abruptly and the left wall peels away to the left. Continue to follow the track as it runs to the right of a fence and by a conifer plantation. It drops down over boggy ground and then climbs steadily south, leaving the forestry behind to emerge on the summit of Kirkhope Law, which is marked by a cairn. Dun Rig is a prominent marker to the southwest.

► Keep the fence to the left as the path descends gradually southwest and maintains this bearing as it climbs over Birkscairn Hill down to a col beneath Stake Law. At this point the drovers would have headed south into the Yarrow Valley. The terrain now begins to become a little boggier, a taster of the muddier conditions that lie ahead.

Continue to follow the fenceposts onto Stake Law, passing to the right of a cairn. Once away from the summit, climb the fence ahead and follow the line of old fenceposts. There are peat hags to cross and the ground can be muddy, so a little meandering in a WSW direction will be required as a steady ascent, eventually running alongside a newer fence, leads onto Dun Rig. Cross a gate on the right to reach the trig point at the summit.

► From the summit pick up an indistinct path that descends north, then northeast down through heather into Glensax. The path leads to a footbridge at the head of the glen just south of Glensax Farm. Turn right onto a track, which soon develops into a minor road, and follow this north through Glensax. Once past Upper Newby the road continues in a northwesterly direction, passing the scattering of houses at Haystoun and then through woodland to return to the start.

The Brown Hill The Scottish landscape is littered with hills with the prefix *Dun*, meaning fort or castle. Dun Da Ghaoithe on Mull, Dun a'Chaisteal in Kintyre and Dumgoyne (in southern Scotland *Dun* often became *Dum*) at the edge of the Campsie Fells are just a few. However, *Dun* also signifies a brown colour and Dun Rig was probably named because of its colour rather than any fort that may have occupied its summit. Whatever the meaning, Dun Rig is an outstanding vantage point to observe the surrounding landscape.

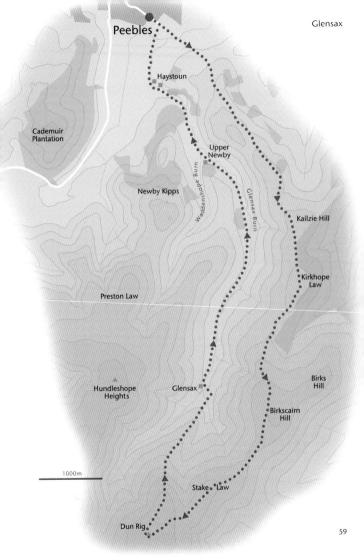

Peebles

Glensax

Cademuir
Plantation

Haystoun

Upper
Newby

Waddenshope Burn

Glensax Burn

Newby Kipps

Kailzie Hill

Kirkhope
Law

Preston Law

Hundleshope
Heights

Glensax

Birks
Hill

Birkscairn
Hill

1000m

Stake Law

Dun Rig

Looking down Glensax from Dun Rig

Preston Law

Hundleshope Heights, Preston Law and Newby Kipps

Distance 12km/7.5 miles
Time 5 hours
Start/Finish Glen Road, Peebles
GR NT259392
Terrain Single-track road, hill and moorland paths and tracks throughout, although good navigational skills may be required in poorer weather. Some steep ascents and descents
Map OS Landranger 73
Public transport Regular First Scotland Service 62 between Edinburgh and Peebles, leaving a walk of around a mile to the start

The celebrated Glensax Horseshoe rising to the south of Peebles is rightly hailed as one of the finest walks in Southern Scotland. To complete the full horseshoe makes for a long day, and so it is far more enjoyable to split the route into two separate walks. A high-level tramp over Glensax's western summits of Hundleshope Heights, Preston Law and Newby Kipps may be less popular than its eastern neighbour (see Walk 9), but it is a wonderful walk in its own right, with excellent paths and a couple of steep ascents connecting these quiet hills.

► From the end of Glen Road, just before the entrance into Gypsy Glen, turn right into a private road (walkers are welcome, vehicles are not), which makes its way south towards Haystoun.

► The road leads through peaceful woodland with great views ahead extending towards the broad flanks of Hundleshope Heights. Keep to the road to pass the scattering of houses at Haystoun and a lovely lochan. The road

The Making of Hay The impressive old mansion house of Haystoun was built in the mid-16th century and then extensively developed in the 17th and 18th centuries when it was the country seat of the Hay Family of Peebles. The name Hay was recorded in 8th-century France, where the Norman family La Haye were followers of the dukes of Normandy, accompanying William the Conqueror to England in 1066 and to Scotland with David I. During the 12th century, William de Haye and his son (also William) served King William the Lion admirably, and in turn were granted the lands of Erroll in Perthshire. The Hays acquired the lands in and around Peebles in the 14th century through marriage into the Fraser Clan, who were the dominant Tweeddale clan of the time.

then continues into Glensax, with the hills of the Glensax Horseshoe enclosing the glen, eventually reaching the farm of Upper Newby.

► Pass by the farm and then a small wood. At this point turn right from the road and climb a steep embankment, keeping the wood to your right, to gain a ridge below the ominously titled Dead Side. Bear left onto a broad, grassy path and follow this as it climbs gradually south and then more steeply onto Dead Side. Even at this modest height (around 450m) the views are superb, particularly north over Peebles and east across the narrow defile of Glensax onto the sharp slopes of Kailzie Hill, Kirkhope Law and Dun Rig, the highest point of the Glensax Horseshoe. The path progresses over Dead Side's lengthy ridge, climbing in a southwesterly direction on an easy and enjoyable section of the walk.

► Continue across a flatter section of moorland, the path cutting through heathery slopes towards Hundleshope Heights, with a final, slightly steeper climb leading to a trig point – the true summit lies a few metres to the west. Hundleshope Heights, at 685m, offers a great view over the Borders and these high, heather-clad peaks are a sanctuary for a wide variety of flora and fauna, including crowberry, blueberry and

tormentil. Red grouse, meadow pipit, wheatear and hen harrier are all migratory visitors.

► From the broad summit descend a faint path northeast to reach a line of grouse butts, which sit on a flatter plateau of moorland. The path then goes left, bearing northwest to arrive at a line of fenceposts. Turn right here and follow the fence as it rises gradually northeast to reach the summit of Preston Law. The northern side of Preston Law is steep and gives a spectacular vantage point towards Newby Kipps and over the nearby Cademuir Hill.

► Continue northeast down the steep path over heathery ground and, about halfway down, cross the fence to pick up another path. Follow the fence (now on the right) and then a wall, and tackle the final climb of the day, up steep slopes onto Newby Kipps, to reach a meeting of walls. The summit of Newby Kipps is perhaps the most fulfilling (and unexpected) part of the day as a small outcrop of rock provides a great vantage point.

► The descent from Newby Kipps is again steep. Cross the wall ahead and then bear right and descend the slope east towards a small patch of woodland. As the ground flattens turn left and

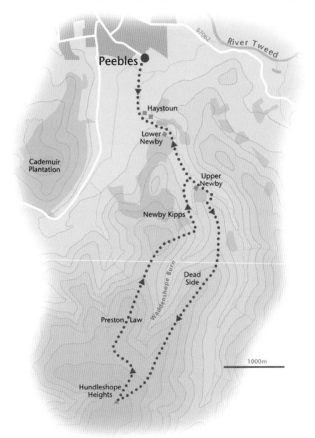

head north towards a break in the trees to pick up a track. Follow this out of the woodland and then continue along the track, passing through a couple of gates and by Upper Newby farm to return to the outward road. Turn left and follow the road through Glensax and past Haystoun to return to Glen Road.

Brown Knowe from Minchmoor

Yarrowford and Minchmoor

Distance 11.5km/7.25 miles
Time 3 hours 30
Start/Finish Yarrowford
GR NT407299
Terrain Single-track road, moorland and woodland paths and tracks
Map OS Landranger 73
Public transport Limited Munros of Jedburgh Service S03 between Selkirk and Yarrowford

The Minchmoor Road is one of the most historic pathways in Scotland and has been travelled by all manner of people – from drovers to kings – over the centuries. Today, the excellent paths and tracks, including a section of the Southern Upland Way, provide a great high-level walk across this picturesque corridor of the Scottish Borders. Dogs should be kept on leads throughout.

► From the phonebox at Yarrowford walk west a short distance and then turn right at a sign for 'Innerleithen via The Minch Moor'. Walk by some houses and go straight on as the road narrows, which then climbs gradually. As it swings left take a rough track on the right. Enter woodland and climb steadily to a fork. Take the right fork and climb above a burn to a gate. Go through this, before turning immediately left onto the lower reaches of Minchmoor Road.

► Follow an initially indistinct field-edge path, running to the right of woodland and a drystone wall, through a gate from where the track becomes more obvious and maintains a steady climb northwest through another two gates. Soon the track swings right away from the woodland and continues between the wall and a fence. Once through another gate carry on along Minchmoor Road with expansive views opening out across the rolling hills.

► After a further gate, the path picks up the line of a wall ascending more steeply and eventually swinging left to contour NNW on the lower slopes of Brown Knowe. The gradient soon eases and travels alongside well-scattered rowan and hawthorn to gain a junction with the Southern Upland Way (SUW).

The King's Highway The Minchmoor Road was once a busy trade route, part of the main highway between the east and west of Scotland. Drovers would regularly use it when driving cattle south to the major tryst at Carlisle. Edward I also travelled on Minchmoor Road when he brought his invading army into Scotland in 1296 and The Marquis of Montrose is thought to have retreated along it, following his defeat at nearby Philiphaugh by the Covenanter Army led by David Leslie in 1645.

► Leave Minchmoor Road by turning right onto the SUW, signposted 'Southern Upland Way to Yair', and follow the excellent high-level track east over the rounded dome of Brown Knowe. Its summit, marked by a small cairn, gives a marvellous 360-degree panorama across the Tweed Valley and over the Borders and Galloway.

► Cross a fence by a stile, where the drove road now threads its way over exposed moorland and then begins to descend to a thin strip of woodland, the final few metres being quite steep. Here, go over a stile and continue southeast alongside a well-maintained wall with the woodland soon left behind. The Cheviot and Eildon Hills form an impressive view as the track drops down over a stile and makes its way around the base of Broomy Law. Cross another stile and then after 100m a sign is reached pointing right for Broadmeadows Youth Hostel.

► Turn right from the SUW, cross a stile and go straight on, following a field-edge path south with a wall to the right. At a fork go right and continue beside the wall as a path descends gradually down into a glen. It soon bears left away from the wall and then descends by a number of waymarkers. Cross over a burn and, once across a second burn, bear left to reach an old farm track. Turn

right and follow this to a waymark beside a pocket of woodland. Turn right, crossing a boardwalk over boggy ground and then a footbridge. Go through a gate, then immediately turn left through another gate onto a lovely path, which descends gently down through birch woodland to Broadmeadows Youth Hostel.

► Turn right around the front of the youth hostel onto a rough road. Follow this down by a cottage and then go through a gate beside a cattle grid. Once through another gate at a cattle grid the road swings left and drops gently by some houses to a junction. Turn left onto a single-track road, which meanders down by more houses and through woodland to reach the main road at Yarrowford. Turn right to return to the phonebox.

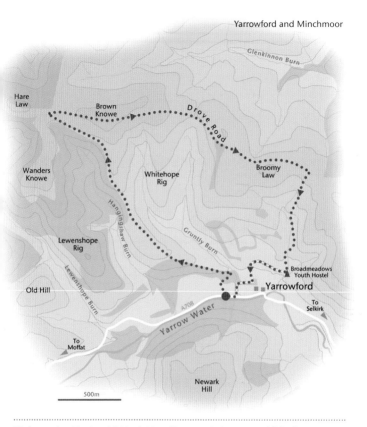

Welcome Inn The Scottish Youth Hostelling Association was established in 1931. Its objective was to provide low-cost accommodation for all, particularly for young people to enable them to experience and appreciate the Scottish countryside, and to promote health, recreation and education.

This coincided with the great working-class outdoor movement of the 1930s. Broadmeadows Youth Hostel became the association's first hostel when it was opened in 1931. Originally a row of four cottages, it was converted and gifted to the SYHA by William Stewart Morton, and offers a stunning view over the Yarrow Valley.

Broadmeadows Youth Hostel

The Borders from the Three Brethren

Philiphaugh and the Three Brethren

Distance **8km/5 miles**
Time **2 hours**
Start/Finish **Philiphaugh car park, on the outskirts of Selkirk GR NT455288**
Terrain **Single-track road, moorland paths and tracks**
Map **OS Landranger 73**
Public transport **Regular First Scotland Service 95 between Edinburgh and Selkirk. Philiphaugh is a little over a mile from Selkirk town centre**

The striking cairns of the Three Brethren occupy a commanding position on the moorland above Selkirk. They present a worthwhile objective for a scenic walk that travels along good moorland paths

and tracks. The path climbs gradually to over 1100ft above sea level and offers an expansive vantage point across much of the Borders. The return journey makes use of a short section of the Southern Upland Way and heads back onto the outward track for a simple walk back to Philiphaugh. Much of the walk crosses farmland, so dogs should be kept on a lead.

► From the car park at Philiphaugh take the farm track on the left, signposted 'Corbie Linn and the Three Brethren'. This broad track climbs gradually and soon veers right to reach a fork. Take the left fork, from where the gradual climb continues northwest

Tweed Town Selkirk is a typical Borders town, built around its marketplace. It developed a reputation for shoemaking in the 15th century and the townsfolk are still known as *souters*, meaning cobblers. However, Selkirk is best known for its textile industry, and by the 19th century the town had seven mills employing more than 1000 people in the production of fine tweeds. Selkirk celebrates its history and traditions during the annual Common Riding, in which up to 500 riders on horseback commemorate their ancestors who protected the borders of the town.

On the outskirts of Selkirk is the site of the Battle of Philiphaugh, which took place on 13 September 1645. It was one of a series of battles that took place between Royalist troops, led by the Marquis of Montrose, and the Covenanters. Montrose had recently won a key battle at Kilsyth and subsequently marched confidently into the Borders, which was a Covenanting stronghold. Montrose was unable to muster enough troops, however, and the Covenanters, led by General David Leslie, won a decisive victory.

alongside woodland, with some fine countryside views. Keep to the main track as it enters a strip of pine woodland and travels above the attractive Long Philip Burn.

► The track soon exits the woodland, swings left and climbs a little more steeply above a ravine and then by Corbie Linn. Where the track reaches another waymarked fork, bear right onto a broad track and follow this as it climbs through another pocket of woodland. Ignore a track descending to the left; instead keep straight on, the track levelling out as it leaves the woodland for wilder countryside. It now follows the course of the Long Philip Burn between a fence and a wall for some time, with the steep slopes of Peat Law and Foulshiels Hill ahead.

► Once past a little reservoir, you come to a stile and a gate. Go over the stile and walk along the track, still keeping beside the burn. When the track sweeps right, carry straight on up a steeper slope and continue with the Three Brethren cairns coming into view ahead.

► After a while, you come to a fork. Take the left branch onto a narrow, grassy path (the main track sweeps away to the right at this point). It is now a long, gradual climb through heather-clad slopes which can be quite boggy at first, although stepping-stones have been laid at the worst points. The path heads northwest and then north, broadening out to a track with some fine views as the Three Brethren are approached. The cairns provide an exceptional viewpoint over much of the Borders, in particular the Tweed Valley and the Eildon Hills, which rise a few miles to the east above Melrose.

► From the Three Brethren, turn right onto the Southern Upland Way and follow the path signposted 'Galashiels' towards Peat Law. The well-maintained path descends gradually alongside a fence on the right with the heathery slopes home to hen harrier and kestrel. The ground soon levels out, passing a small conifer plantation, to reach a signpost for 'Selkirk via the Long Philip Burn'. Turn right from the Southern Upland Way here and cross a stile, ignoring a broad track on the left. Instead go straight on and follow a solid track as it traverses around the slopes of Peat Law with Foulshiels Hill ahead.

► The track eventually drops down to reach the outward track. Bear left onto this and retrace your steps to Philiphaugh car park, enjoying good views over the little reservoir towards the hills above Selkirk.

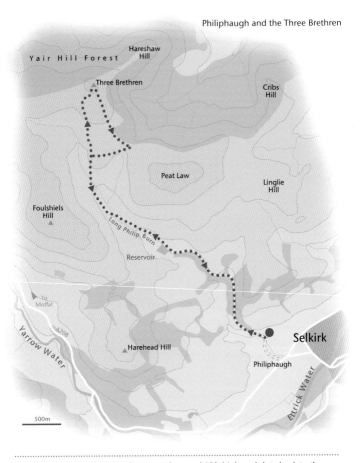

Meeting Place The Three Brethren stand around 10ft high and date back to the 1500s – local lairds built them to mark the boundaries of the ancient burghs of Selkirk, Yair and Philiphaugh. It is said that they signify the meeting of the three great rivers of the Tweed, the Yarrow and the Ettrick, which cut their way around the flanks of moorland beneath the Three Brethren.

Langlee Woodland

Gala Hill and Langlee

Distance 9km/5.5 miles
Time 3 hours
Start/Finish Livingstone Place,
Galashiels NT488359
Terrain Pavement, woodland and
riverside paths, golf course. Some
steep ascents and descents
Map OS Landranger 73
Public transport Regular First
Scotland Service 95 between
Edinburgh and Galashiels

**This is a fine circuit around
Galashiels, taking in a broad range
of walking terrain including the
slopes of Gala Hill, a great vantage
point to enjoy wonderful views over
the Borders, Gala Policies and
Langlee Woodland, home to a
magnificent array of flora and fauna.**

► From the car park on Livingstone
Place in Galashiels, go through a gate
onto a track signposted 'Gala Policies
Southern Upland Way'. The track
immediately forks. Go left, following this
fine woodland track beside a burn and
the High School.

► At a crossroads beside a small pond,
go straight on over a wooden footbridge
and continue to a junction. Turn left,
then next right where the path strikes
through the oak and beech woodland.
Pass a signpost for 'Gala Hill Southern
Upland Way' to a gate.

► Beyond the gate, turn left (leaving
the SUW), follow the path over a
wooden footbridge and then left
through a gate at a Galashiels Path
waymark. Climb along a woodland path
which traverses the lower slopes of Gala
Hill (southeast). At a fork go right and,
upon reaching a single-track road, cross
over, go through a gate and follow the
steep path around Gala Hill. At the next
fork go left to climb the path to another
fork. Go left again and follow the path
as it swings right, exiting the woodland
beside two gates. There are some fine
views from here and it is alleged that
the Earl of Dunbar sought refuge on
this hill from William Wallace in the
12th century.

► Take the right-hand gate into a field,
turn left and descend the field edge to a
wall. Turn right, back onto the SUW,
walking alongside the wall to a gate on
the left. Go through here into another

Town Assets The local council
purchased Gala Policies Community
Woodland in 1974. The woodland was
once part of a much larger estate owned
by Hugh Scott, Laird of Galashiels, who
married into the famous Pringle family
of Gala. The woodland is home to native
and foreign tree species, such as ancient
oaks thought to have formed part of the
original Ettrick Forest, Norway maple
and giant redwood.

field where a broad farm track drops down through one more gate and past Brunswickhill House. A rough road descends to Abbotsford Road. Cross Abbotsford Road, turning right and then left onto a paved path which descends a flight of steps to reach the A7. Carefully cross here, turning right and then left onto a single-track road, signposted for Selkirk, which drops down through a gate and then over a bridge. Bear left at a SUW post to follow a path over a single-track road to the banks of the River Tweed.

► On this section, a wooded riverside path gives great views across the Tweed to Abbotsford House. Climb a flight of steps and continue above the river. The path then drops gently to pass by a small car park and then underneath Galafoot Bridge. Go straight on along an area of parkland, swing left at the outflow of the Gala Water and, after passing through a gate, bear right to pass through a short strip of woodland, exiting via a gate onto Winston Road. Cross Winston Road, turn right and follow the pavement over the Gala Water, leaving behind the SUW to gain Melrose Road (B6374).

► Cross Melrose Road, turn right to follow the pavement over Eildon Lodge Gardens and then turn left onto a path just before Easter Langlee Industrial Estate. Climb the path between trees and a wire fence and, once away from the fence, turn left onto a woodland path and continue to a waymark. Turn right to follow a path as it climbs gradually by some houses and over a crossroads. It then rises steeply to a fork. Take the right branch and carry on through the woodland to eventually reach a clearing, where your exertions are rewarded with great views of the Eildon Hills.

► Descend to a fork, turning right and then left onto a narrow path which climbs alongside a fence to a fork. Again go right and follow the waymarked posts by a transmission mast, after which a sharp descent takes you to another path. Turn right, continue to follow the waymarks and, where the path splits, again go right, eventually dropping down a flight of steps and turning right to a gate. Go through the gate, cross a minor road and then pass through another gate into Langlee Community Woodland.

► An excellent path ascends out of the wood to a fork. Take the left branch for a section on a great high-level path with some fine views over Gala. This is followed through a gate and, once through a gap in an old wall, turn left and descend a grassy path over Galashiels Golf Course to meet a narrow road beside the clubhouse.

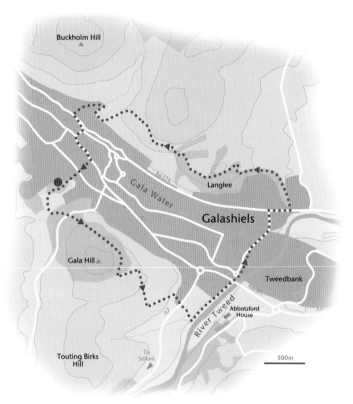

▶ Walk down the road, turning right at a junction onto a path. Walk around a barrier and then turn left over a bridge, crossing the Ladhope Burn. Keep straight on to Heatheryett Drive, turn left and descend to High Buckholmside (A7). Turn left and then right onto Bridge Place, to cross the Gala Water.

▶ Turn left onto High Street, following the pavement onto Bank Street and then right onto Livingstone Place to return to the start.

Bluebell

Red Campion

Buttercup field

Galashiels and Ladhope

Distance 5.5km/3.5 miles
Time 1 hour 30
Start/Finish Livingstone Place, Galashiels NT488359
Terrain Pavement, woodland and moorland paths, golf course. Some steep ascents and descents
Map OS Landranger 73
Public transport Regular First Scotland Service 95 between Edinburgh and Galashiels

This short walk over the high ground above Galashiels is the perfect way to introduce younger kids to a tougher walk without taking them too far out of their comfort zone. Good paths line the route, which climbs steeply above the town to give fantastic views.

▶ From the car park at the top of Livingstone Place descend to Bank Street, turn left, continue onto High Street and then turn right onto Bridge Place. Follow the pavement over the Gala Water, then turn left onto High Buckholmside (A7). Walk by High Road, then turn right onto Ladhope Drive. After walking along the pavement for

20m, turn left onto a gravel path. Follow this to a fork, bearing right to take a woodland path across a footbridge and up two flights of steps to meet a paved path, signposted 'Ladhope Recreation Ground'.

▶ Turn right, crossing a bridge over the Ladhope Burn, then bear right along the path around a barrier to reach a single-track road. Turn left to climb the steep road to Galashiels Golf Club. Go straight on by the clubhouse onto a track and then bear right onto the fairway. Walk past a Galashiels Path marker post where a grassy path ascends steeply through the golf course. Go straight on by a green and an old wall, leaving the golf course behind, onto another grassy path, which immediately branches.

▶ Take the left fork, climbing the steep path over grassland and then through gorse-covered hillside. Terrific views across Galashiels to Meigle Hill quickly open up. The gradient eases as the path continues across an area of grassland to a fork at a marker post. Bear left for a more gradual descent through more gorse to return to the golf course at a

Leisure Centre Ladhope Recreation Ground was gifted to the residents of Galashiels by local landowners in 1913. The development of Galashiels Golf Club commenced a year later – James Braid, the renowned golfer and golf course architect, designed the course. Ladhope quickly became popular with locals for walking, something which has endured because of the fantastic views and vast array of wildlife.

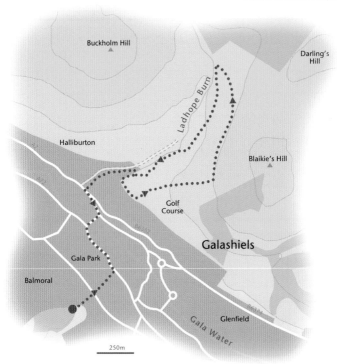

crossroads. Turn left where a good path skirts the edge of the golf course back towards Gala.

► Once by a green and over a low ramshackle wall, the path drops steeply and runs alongside a conifer wood to reach an old well on the left. At this point turn right, carefully crossing to the other side of the golf course, and turn left onto another path. Walk along the edge of the course to reach a waymarked post. Turn right from the golf course down a flight of wooden steps and into woodland above the Ladhope Burn. The path leads you back to the outward route, where you turn right to cross the bridge back over the Ladhope Burn and then retrace your steps into Galashiels.

Galashiels from Ladhope

Melrose and Gattonside

Distance 6.75km/4.25 miles
Time 1 hour 30
Start/Finish Market Square, Melrose
GR NT558340
Terrain Pavement, riverside paths,
countryside tracks, single-track road
Map OS Landranger 73
Public transport Limited direct
National Express Service 534
between Glasgow, Edinburgh
and Melrose

An assortment of paths, tracks
and roads circumnavigate the
River Tweed from Melrose to
visit the quiet villages of Darnick
and Gattonside. Lowood Bridge
and the Gattonside Suspension
Bridge are crossed during the walk.

► Leave Market Square by walking
along Abbey Street, then turn left
at Melrose Abbey onto Buccleuch
Street. Walk along the pavement before
bearing right onto High Street and
continuing by Greenyards. After St
Mary's Road, High Street becomes High
Cross Avenue, which you continue to
follow left at a fork and on into Darnick.

Follow Abbotsford Road through
the village's narrow streets to reach
Waverley Road (B6374). Carefully cross
the road onto a lane to the left of
Waverley Castle Hotel. This leads down
by a cottage onto a grassy track where
you then go through a gate to reach the
River Tweed. Turn left and follow a
lovely riverside path with the impressive
archways of Lowood Bridge ahead. The
path climbs a flight of steps and goes
through a gate to climb past Skirmish
Hill (see Walk 16), continuing through
another gate to reach the B6374.

► Turn right down the B6374 and
carefully cross the Lowood Bridge (there
is no pavement) over the Tweed. Take
the first right (B6360), signposted
Gattonside, where a pavement climbs
gently above the Tweed. Once past a
cottage on the left, cross the road onto a
waymarked Southern Upland Way path.
Walk up this rough track to reach a
minor road.

► Turn right (leaving the SUW) and
follow this quiet road by Gattonmains
Farm, enjoying views of Melrose and the

Seven Heaven Greenyards is the home of the famous Melrose Rugby Club, and the
internationally renowned Melrose Rugby Sevens. The club was formed in 1877, and
has won the First Division Championship on several occasions. Melrose has
provided many internationalists, including players of the calibre of Craig Chalmers
and Jim Telfer. The Melrose Sevens tournament is played on the second Saturday of
every April, and regularly attracts crowds in excess of 10,000.

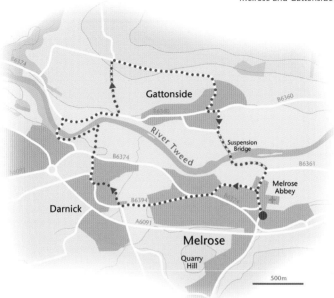

Eildon Hills. After the farm, the road drops gently down through the village of Gattonside which, after being gifted to Melrose Abbey in 1143 by King David I, became the abbey's orchard.

Access Point The impressive Gattonside Suspension Bridge was opened in 1826 providing access between Melrose and Gattonside. There was also a ford further downstream for horse-drawn vehicles. In those days conditions placed upon using the bridge meant that no more than eight people were allowed on it at any one time, and it was a statutory offence to make the bridge swing.

▶ Descend The Loan, bearing right at a fork to return to the B6360. Cross the road, turning left and then right onto Hoebridge Road East. Follow the pavement down to a fork. Turn left onto Bridge Street and continue to reach Gattonside Suspension Bridge spanning the River Tweed.

▶ Cross the bridge, turn left onto Chain Bridge Road and walk along to Annay Road (B6361). Turn right, follow the pavement onto Abbey Street and continue back to Market Square and your start point.

Market Square, Melrose

Lowood Bridge, Melrose

Melrose and Abbotsford

Distance 9.5km/6 miles
Time 2 hours 30
Start/Finish Market Square, Melrose
GR NT558340
Terrain Pavement, riverside paths,
single-track road
Map OS Landranger 73
Public transport Limited direct
National Express Service 534 between
Glasgow, Edinburgh and Melrose

The history and landscape of the
Scottish Borders has inspired some of
the great writers and poets. A walk
from Melrose to Abbotsford and back
illustrates this perfectly. Melrose
Abbey and Abbotsford House, the
home of Sir Walter Scott for much of
his life, are visited on a scenic and
tranquil route that takes advantage
of the superb Borders Abbeys Way.

► Leave Market Square by walking
down Abbey Street and past the
magnificent Melrose Abbey. Continue by
the National Trust for Scotland property
of Harmony Garden and then turn left
onto Chain Bridge Road. Follow this to
reach Gattonside Suspension Bridge. Go
straight on past the bridge onto a paved
path beside the River Tweed, signposted
Borders Abbeys Way (BAW). After around
50m the path swings left (signposted
Melrose Town Centre). Ignore this;
instead go straight on along a grassy
path to climb a flight of steps onto a

paved path. This travels above the
Tweed, initially alongside a wall and a
fence, before descending gently through
mixed woodland to a road.

► Turn right, pass a gate and continue
for a few metres to a second gate. Turn
right through the gate onto a broad,
grassy track which immediately forks.
Either grassy track can be taken as they
run parallel to one another alongside
the Tweed until they converge at a stone
bridge. Cross the bridge from which
point a single track continues along the
Tweed, passing through a gate, with the
Lowood Bridge eventually coming into
view. The path then climbs a flight of
steps, passes through another gate and
then climbs by Skirmish Hill, the site of a

Monastic Order Melrose Abbey was
established in 1136 by David I, and was
the first Cistercian monastery to be built
in Scotland. The fertile lands surrounding
the River Tweed encouraged the
Cistercian monks of Rievaulx in Yorkshire
to settle there. The last resident monk
died at Melrose around 1590.
Many privileges were bestowed on the
abbey, but it also drew unwanted
attention. Edward I and Edward II
attacked in the early 14th century,
whilst Richard II's assault in 1385 meant
the abbey church had to be completely
rebuilt. Melrose Abbey is thought to be
where Robert the Bruce's heart is buried.

battle that took place here in 1526 between Archibald Douglas, Walter Scott of Buccleuch and around 1600 of their supporters. Follow the path through a gate to reach the B6374.

► Turn right to follow the pavement down to Lowood Bridge. Don't cross the bridge; instead cross the road and go straight on to the driveway for Lowood House. Walk along the driveway before turning right at a BAW signpost onto a path. This descends gently through mixed woodland to reach the banks of the Tweed. The riverside path leads you through beautiful countryside for approximately 0.75 miles to arrive at an old railway bridge on the outskirts of Galashiels (now a cycle/walkway).

► Go through a gate to pass beneath the bridge, walk past a BAW signpost and, at a second post, bear right onto a woodland path. This continues along the Tweed, passing over some sections of boardwalk. Once over a footbridge, follow the BAW waymarkers, bearing right at a fork and then left at the next fork. The path sweeps right to reach a paved path which you bear right onto for a gentle ascent by some houses with good views over the Tweed to Galashiels.

► Just before the A6091 leave the path at a BAW post and bear right down a flight of steps, passing underneath the Galafoot Road Bridge and then climbing steps to the other side of the bridge. A path descends through woodland before turning left to rise gradually to reach the B6360 beside Abbotsford House.

► To continue the walk, cross the B6360 onto a narrow waymarked road. It rises quite steeply through more woodland and, after a while, swings left by some farm buildings. The gradient eases where the road carries

Great Scott Sir Walter Scott is one of Scotland's greatest writers, the author of *Waverley*, *Ivanhoe*, *Rob Roy* and *The Lady of the Lake*. A visit to Abbotsford House is a must for anyone with an interest in architecture, design and literature. In 1811, Sir Walter Scott bought the property upon which Abbotsford House would be built. He designed and oversaw the extension of what was originally a farmhouse into the beautiful building we see today. It was completed in 1824. Unlike Burns, Scott lived to enjoy his success, which allowed him to decorate the interiors of the house to his taste. He filled the rooms with an incredible collection of historic relics, and an extensive library with more than 9000 rare books. Abbotsford House was opened to the public in 1833, and is a major visitor attraction.

on to pass a road on the right – this is where the Borders Abbeys Way is left behind. It then drops gently through Kaeside Farm (watch out for farm traffic), passes by Sunnyside Farm and heads towards Darnick with some superb views of the Eildons. Cross the A6091 by a bridge onto Broomilees Road and into the village of Darnick.

► Turn right onto Abbotsford Road (B6394) and head through Darnick onto High Cross Avenue. Walk along the pavement back into Melrose. At a junction, turn right (still High Cross Avenue) and follow this onto High Street, passing Greenyards (home of Melrose Rugby Club), to return to Market Square.

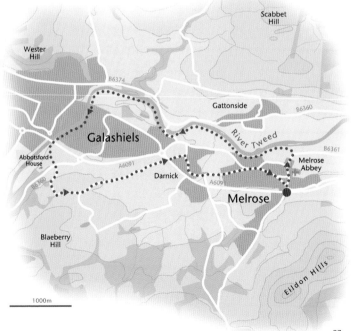

Melrose Abbey

Abbotsford

Melrose and the Tweed from the Eildon Hills

The Eildon Hills

Distance **8.25km/5 miles**
Time **4 hours**
Start/Finish **Market Square, Melrose GR NT558340**
Terrain **Pavement, countryside paths and tracks, hill paths with several steep ascents**
Map **OS Landranger 73**
Public transport **Limited direct National Express Service 534 between Glasgow, Edinburgh and Melrose**

The Eildon Hills may not be the highest in the Scottish Borders, but make no mistake – their slopes are steep. There are several tough climbs throughout this walk, although it is made slightly easier by the excellent paths and tracks that criss-cross this wonderful little range of hills.

► From Market Square walk down Abbey Street and, just before Melrose Abbey, turn right onto Priorswalk. Follow this lane by the abbey and then onto a paved path through a park. Once over a footbridge bear left at a fork, following a Borders Abbeys Way sign, and continue by some houses to reach a pavement. Walk along the pavement – this is still Priorswalk – and, as it swings right, turn left onto a waymarked path. Go through a gate onto a grassy path and walk along this for around half a mile to reach a gate beside Dean Road at Newstead.

► Beyond the gate, turn left onto Dean Road and then right onto a Borders Abbeys Way (BAW) path, which rises gradually through woodland, veering left to reach a waymarked junction. Following the BAW waymarks, turning right to go under a railway bridge, through a gate and under the A6091. The path then swings right and rises to meet the A6091. Turn left to reach two metal gates. Go through the left gate onto a wide track, which then climbs gradually alongside hedgerows to gain a minor road.

Ancient Town Melrose was originally recorded in the 8th century as *Mailros* (Cumbric), meaning 'the Bare Moor'. The Eildon Hills overlook the town, which owes its existence to Melrose Abbey. The distinctive ruin of the abbey is probably the most famous in Scotland (see Walk 16 for more information). The association between Melrose and monastic life dates back several centuries before Melrose Abbey was established, when St Aidan founded a monastery nearby in around 650AD. During the 15th and 16th centuries, wool and linen played an important role in Melrose's development, although today tourism is vital to the economy of this lovely town. A little east of Melrose is Newstead, reputedly the oldest inhabited village in Scotland.

► Turn right (leaving the BAW), walk down the road for a few metres, then turn left onto a path which climbs through woodland to a gate. Go through the gate, bear left at a fork and ascend the path onto Eildon North Hill's lower slopes. Here the path rises very steeply southwest over open hillside with around 200m of height to be gained pretty rapidly. The gradient only relents as the summit is approached. The path continues gently for the final few metres to attain the cairn on the summit of North Hill.

► From the top, take the right of three paths, which drops southwest to a fork. Bear right to follow the track towards the base of Mid Hill, bearing right onto another track and then left at a fork. At the next track go left, then right at a St Cuthbert's Way sign onto a narrow path which makes its way southwest around the lower slopes of Mid Hill. Follow this above some woodland to reach a col between Mid and Wester Hill. Cross a track (beside a Melrose Paths post) and then swing right onto the next track. Follow this to reach the summit of Wester Hill, a fine spot to look south across the Borders towards the Cheviots and Galloway Hills.

► Retrace your steps down to reach the crossroads beside the Melrose Paths marker. Turn left and follow the track towards Little Hill. At a waymark take the right fork and go right again at the next fork to pass Little Hill. At another marker turn right onto a path, which climbs steeply to the 422m summit of Mid Hill, the highest point of the Eildons. The surrounding landscape is so flat that the panorama extends for miles; on a clear day the Lake District hills are visible.

► Continue by the trig point with the path then swinging left and zigzagging steeply back down to the col between North and Mid Hill. Go straight on at a crossroads and then turn left onto St Cuthbert's Way. The path descends gradually north around North Hill, eventually dropping down a flight of

Home on the Range Local folklore suggests that a legendary wizard, Michael Scot, created the distinctive shape of the Eildons by splitting one hill into three. Long before the Romans set up camp, the Eildons were utilised by the locals as a place of refuge. The Old English translation simply means 'Old Hill Fort', and around the time of the Bronze Age it is thought that up to 2000 people lived on the Eildons, predominantly on the flat-topped North Hill.

The Romans occupied the Eildon Hills and built a signal station here around 3AD, naming them Trimontium, which translates as the 'Three Mountains'.

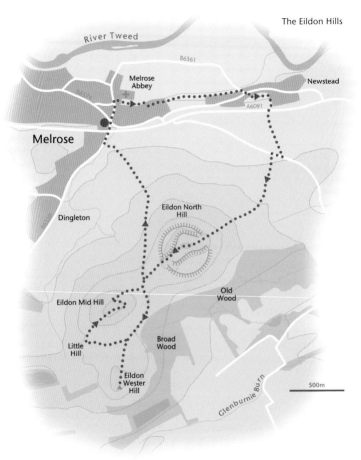

wooden steps to a gate. Go through here, following a fenced track down through two more gates onto another fenced path, which descends to a stile. Go over the stile, walk down a long flight of wooden steps and then cross a footbridge over a burn. Climb a flight of stone steps to reach Dingleton Road. Turn right and walk down the pavement back to Market Square.

The Eildon Hills

William Wallace statue

Newtown St Boswells and Dryburgh Abbey

Distance 12.5km/7.75 miles
Time 3 hours
Start/Finish Earlston Road, Newtown St Boswells GR NT576317
Terrain Pavement, single-track road, woodland and riverside paths
Map OS Landranger 74
Public transport Regular Munros of Jedburgh Service 51 between Edinburgh and Newtown St Boswells

Perhaps the finest of the four Scottish Border Abbeys is Dryburgh Abbey, which is situated near to the charming village of Newtown St Boswells. The well-maintained St Cuthbert's Way and the Borders Abbeys Way paths provide easy walking along the Tweed to visit the Abbey. A short distance off the main route, a path climbs to reach a statue commemorating Scotland's celebrated freedom fighter.

▶ Facing the Scottish Borders Council Offices on Earlston Road (B6398) turn left, walk through the village and go left onto Tweedside Road. Follow the road and then turn left at a St Cuthbert's Way (SCW) and Borders Abbeys Way (BAW) sign onto a single-track road for a gentle descent. Just before passing underneath a roadbridge, turn right onto a waymarked path and follow this underneath the bridge into woodland. Continue over the Bowden Burn via a footbridge, keeping straight on at a fork, from where the path eventually climbs three flights of steps in quick succession. Once over a footbridge swing right to cross another footbridge. Stay on the path until it drops down steps onto a minor road.

▶ Turn left, leave the SCW and cross a green suspension bridge over the Tweed, signposted 'Dryburgh Abbey and Wallace Statue', to join the BAW. Turn right, passing the Temple of the Muses, a distinctive monument to Borders poet James Thomson. Walk

The Not So New Town Although the name implies otherwise, the village of Newtown St Boswells dates back to medieval times when it was a centre for milling grain.

Over the years it has been called Newtoun, Newton, Newtown of Eildon and Newtown of Dryburgh. It was in 1849, when the Edinburgh & Hawick Railway decided to name a new railway station Newtown St Boswells (after St Boisil, who had been an abbot at Melrose Abbey), that the village acquired the same name. The nearby village of Lesludden was also renamed as St Boswells.

along a single-track road to a junction. Turn left onto a road (leaving the BAW), walk along the verge, passing several houses, and climb to a path on the left signposted 'Wallace's Statue'. Take the path to climb steeply through pleasant woodland to another signpost. Turn right and follow another path to reach Wallace's Statue, which enjoys an excellent outlook over the shapely Eildon Hills.

► Retrace your steps down to the road, turn right and keep on the road as it descends onto the BAW to arrive at Dryburgh Abbey.

► Walk through the car park and then bear left by the visitor toilets onto a narrow road. Just before reaching a gate at a private road turn left by a BAW sign, cross a stile, follow a wide grassy track and continue over another stile to a fork. Take the waymarked right branch and follow the riverside track as it progresses through some glorious countryside, eventually reaching a wood. Here, the path turns left and then immediately right to rise above the Tweed and continue its course through the woodland. When the track swings left go straight on to a gate. Go through the gate, follow a path for approximately 50m, then turn right over a stile, leaving the BAW behind.

► A flight of steps descends to the Tweed and onto an indistinct grassy path, which passes around the front of some cottages towards Mertoun Bridge. Once by the cottages turn left, cross a footbridge and then turn right to reach Mertoun Bridge. Turn right onto the B6404 and carefully cross the bridge (no pavement) back over the Tweed. Once across the bridge immediately turn right down steps back onto St Cuthbert's Way.

► Initially the path hugs the banks of the River Tweed, then runs along the left edge of St Boswells Golf Course. Follow the path along its length (where golf etiquette must be observed) to reach a waymarked single-track road. Turn left and climb the steep road by St Boswells Clubhouse to reach Braeheads Road.

River Retreat A visit to the majestic remains of Dryburgh Abbey is a must. The building stands alone, surrounded on three sides by the meandering River Tweed – an appropriately beautiful and peaceful spot. The abbey was established in 1150 when the chief local landowner, Hugh de Morville, invited the Premonstratensian monks of Alnwick Abbey in Northumberland to settle here. Work on Dryburgh Abbey continued over the next 150 years, but Edward II and his army destroyed much of the building in 1322.

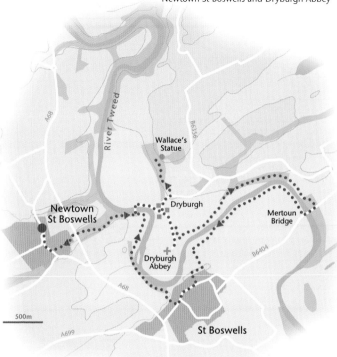

Turn right to walk along the road, with superb views of the Eildons – this turns left and descends into St Boswells. Turn right onto Main Street and follow the pavement through the village to reach Hamilton Place at a SCW sign.

▶ Turn right along Hamilton Place, bearing right at a fork and then left onto a waymarked path which drops gradually through woodland, crossing a footbridge to return to the Tweed. The path ascends and descends a flight of steps, then sticks to the Tweed for easy navigation, returning to the green suspension bridge after just under a mile. Cross the road and climb the steps back onto the outward route before retracing your steps into Newtown St Boswells.

Dryburgh Abbey

Eildon Hills from Newtown St Boswells

Smailholm and Smailholm Tower

Distance 6.25km/3.75 miles
Time 1 hour 30
Start/Finish Smailholm Village
GR NT649364
Terrain Pavement, minor road,
roadside verge, farm tracks, grassy
path. Route passes over farmland, so
keep dogs on leads
Map OS Landranger 74
Public transport First Scotland East
Service 166 from Galashiels and
Kelso to Smailholm

The 15th-century Smailholm Tower
is the focal point to this scenic walk
that begins and ends at the peaceful
village of Smailholm. The views are
wonderful throughout, particularly
from Smailholm Tower's hilltop
location. Although the simplest
return route is to retrace your steps,
there is a more rewarding circular
journey; however, this requires
walking along a roadside verge for
just under a mile.

▶ Facing Smailholm Church on the
B6397 at Smailholm, turn right and go
straight on as the road forks onto the
Smailholm/Leaderfoot road. Walk
through Smailholm to a road signposted
for Smailholm Tower. Turn left and
follow this quiet country road as it
twists and turns through the landscape,
granting some exquisite views across
the Tweed Valley and the Borders.

▶ At a fork in the road follow the
signpost for Smailholm Tower. The road
climbs gently by Miens Plantation and
then through Sandyknowes Farm. At
another fork go right, passing through
a gate beside a cattle grid onto a
rougher track. Climb the track, with the
outline of Smailholm Tower sitting on
the rocky outcrop ahead. Once by an
old millpond and just before a car park,

High Society Smailholm Tower is a peel
tower – a defensive towerhouse – that
commands stunning views of the
surrounding countryside. The tower is all
that remains of what was once a
flourishing settlement. Cottages, livestock
enclosures, stables and a mill are just
some of the buildings that would have
surrounded it.

The tower was built by the Pringles, a
leading Borders family, in the mid-15th
century. Because of its close proximity to
the Scottish/English border, raiders
attacked it many times over the
subsequent years; these attacks only
stopped when the Pringles agreed
not to participate in raids on English soil.
Sir Walter Scott spent time at Smailholm
Tower as a small child – it had been sold
to the Scott family during the
17th century. The towerhouse is now
under the care of Historic Scotland,
and is open daily between April and
September and at weekends between
October and March.

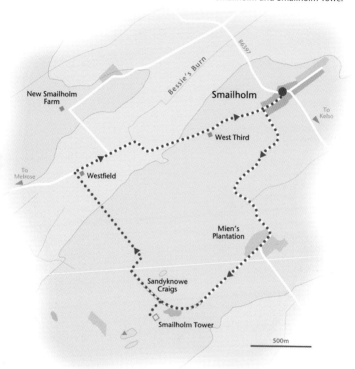

turn left from the track onto a grassy slope. Keeping the tower to the left, climb gradually around it to reach its entrance gate.

► Retrace your steps to the track, turning left to go past the car park and through a gate. The track swings right through another gate before bearing left through a third gate onto a field-edge

track. Follow this northwest as it descends gently, returning to the Smailholm/Leaderfoot road beside Westfield Cottages. Go through a gate, turn right and keep along the verge, enjoying further fine rural views. The road sweeps right, then left back into Smailholm. Once by the Smailholm Tower access road, continue back to Smailholm Church.

Smailholm Tower

Farmland near Roxburgh

Kelso and Roxburgh

Distance 10.5km/6.5 miles
Time 3 hours
**Start/Finish The Square, Kelso
GR NT727339**
**Terrain Pavement, single-track
roads, woodland, parkland and
riverside paths**
Map OS Landranger 74
**Public transport Munros of
Jedburgh Service 52 between
Edinburgh and Kelso**

The village of Roxburgh used to be
one of the most important trading
towns in Scotland and Roxburgh
Castle was an important defensive
site. This wonderful circular walk
travels along a section of Kelso's
other great river, the Teviot, to visit
both Roxburgh Castle and its village.
The return journey makes its way
along the line of an old railway,
granting some beautiful views.

► Facing the Town Hall on The Square
(see Walk 21 for more information),
turn right and make your way along the
cobble-stoned Bridge Street by Kelso
Abbey. Follow the pavement over
Rennie's Bridge, which is at the junction
of the River Tweed and the River Teviot.
Their convergence forms a deep pool
known as the Junction Pool, and this
union provides some of the best salmon
fishing in Scotland.

► Once over the bridge turn right onto
the A699. The pavement runs alongside
the River Tweed and then swings left by
Springwood Park and right over the River
Teviot by a stone roadbridge. Carry on
along the A699 past a small car park and
a cottage. At the end of a wall turn left
over a stone stile and right onto a path,
then drop down a flight of steps to reach
the Teviot.

► The path progresses easily southwest
along the River Teviot and the Borders
Abbeys Way (BAW), and soon passes the
remains of Roxburgh Castle, which sits on
top of an embankment on the right.
Continuing along the faster-flowing
Teviot, beautiful rural views extend for
miles. Soon the path runs alongside field
edges and this carries on until a stile is
reached after approximately 1.25 miles.

....

Fishy Tales The River Teviot begins its
journey on the slopes of Comb Hill on
the border with Dumfries & Galloway.
The Teviot is one of the main tributaries
of the Tweed and is one of Scotland's
finest rivers for salmon, trout and
grayling fishing. More than 700 salmon
can be taken in a season, with an
average weight of around ten pounds.
As the Teviot approaches Kelso the
riverbank is lined with larch, sycamore,
oak, horse chestnut and common alder.
Wildlife includes kingfisher, goldeneye,
grey heron, swans and otter.

Turn right here, signposted Borders Abbeys Way, and then left to follow another field-edge path with a fence to the left. After a while, this swings right and then left over another stile. Cross another field and go over a final stile onto a minor road.

► Turn left and follow the road down through Roxburgh Mill Farm and then into the village of Roxburgh. Before the centre of the village is reached, turn left onto a narrow road, signposted Borders Abbeys Way, which drops down onto a rougher track signposted 'Ferry Road'. Follow this as it swings right to reach an impressive viaduct spanning the River Teviot.

► Turn left, leaving the BAW, and cross a wooden bridge beside the viaduct to then climb a path which gains a minor road. Turn right, pass under the viaduct and follow the road as it swings left to reach a path on the left signposted 'Kelso 2½ miles'.

► Follow this path for a short distance and, before it veers left, turn right onto a dismantled railway bed. Walk along this excellent hawthorn-lined track as it heads north and then northwest. The expansive views this gives extend to Floors Castle and the Eildon Hills. After around 1.5 miles the track passes the 12th-century farmhouse of Maisondieu – once an asylum for pilgrims, the sickly and the poor.

► Here, the track drops down and, as it swings left, go through a wooden gate on the right and turn left. Follow a woodland path, which swings right to a gate on the left. Go through the gate and walk along a path over a field through a gap in a fence. Turn right, where a narrow path then reaches a broader track.

Roxburgh No More In the Middle Ages, Roxburgh was Scotland's most important royal burgh and the site of a great castle. During the 1120s Roxburgh Castle became the chosen seat of King David I, and it remained the residence of Scottish kings for the next two centuries. Roxburgh and its castle prospered, but ultimately its defences weren't strong enough and it changed hands many times over the next three centuries, eventually falling to the English. In 1460, King James II laid siege to Roxburgh Castle in an attempt to regain it – but not without cost. A cannon exploded, blowing the King's leg off and causing him to bleed to death. The Scots continued the siege until they seized control a few days later. However, over the next few decades Roxburgh Castle was demolished and the community that had built up around it slowly faded away. Little remains of the castle today.

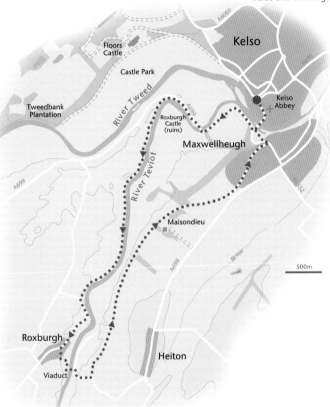

▶ Turn right again and keep on this track, which sometimes has deep puddles along its length, until it eventually reaches Jedburgh Road on the outskirts of Kelso. Turn left, descending Jedburgh Road to the B6352 at a roundabout. Turn left and, after 20m, turn right into Bridgend Park at the Millennium Viewpoint. Drop down a flight of steps, walk through the park and climb the steps back to Bridge Street. Turn right, crossing Rennie's Bridge to return to The Square.

River Teviot

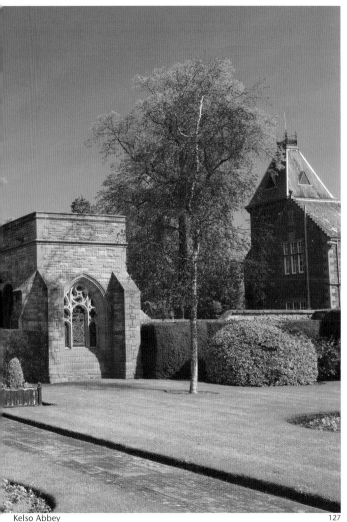

Kelso Abbey

Kelso Abbey

Kelso and Kelso Abbey

Distance 3.5km/2.25 miles
Time 1 hour
Start/Finish The Square, Kelso
GR NT727339
Terrain Pavement, woodland and riverside paths
Map OS Landranger 74
Public transport Munros of Jedburgh Service 52 between Edinburgh and Kelso

Kelso is a charming, lively town, which has a history dating back to the early 12th century. Built along the banks of the River Tweed and around its abbey, Kelso has many fine buildings within the town centre. A selection of town, woodland and riverside paths are combined in this short walk.

► Start the walk from The Square, which is the largest market square in Scotland and is dominated by the striking sandstone façade of the Town Hall, which was built in 1816 to replace the old Tolbooth. Also outside the Town Hall are bullrings, which farmers used to tether their animals on market days. Facing the Town Hall (which is now home to the town's tourist information centre and registrar's office), turn right and make your way along the cobble-stoned Bridge Street and past Kelso Abbey.

► Follow the pavement over Rennie's Bridge, which spans the River Tweed, with some marvellous views to Floors Castle. Rennie's Bridge was built between 1800 and1804 by John Rennie of East Linton and was a prototype for

Power and Influence In its heyday Kelso Abbey was one of the richest in Scotland, its wealth generated by its vast Borders estates. It was founded by King David I in 1128 and was the first and biggest of his Border Abbeys, taking 75 years to build. The other Border abbeys are Melrose, Dryburgh and Jedburgh. During the 12th and 13th centuries, the Abbot of Kelso was granted the right to wear the mitre, making him more powerful than any other Scottish abbot. King James III was crowned at Kelso Abbey in 1460.

Its wealth, power and close proximity to the English Border meant it came under constant close scrutiny from marauding English armies during the Wars of Independence, and the abbey suffered greatly at the start of the 1300s. It was repaired, but was attacked again by the Duke of Hertford and his army in 1542, 1544 and 1545. Like many of Scotland's abbeys, the Reformation of 1560 was the final chapter for Kelso. Between 1650 and 1770 the abbey became a parish church and school, before much of the stone was used in buildings within the town.

Waterloo Bridge in London, also designed by Rennie. Once over the bridge, turn left down a flight of steps into the attractive Bridgend Park. Follow a path straight through the park and then climb a steep flight of steps to reach the Millennium Viewpoint, which provides a fantastic view across the town.

► Leave the park by turning left onto the B6352. Follow the pavement as it climbs by a roundabout and then turn left onto Sprouston Road. Walk along the quiet street, crossing over Abbey View and, as the pavement dips, turn left at a cottage through two stone gateposts. Immediately turn left through a gate onto a woodland path, which drops gently down a flight of steps and travels to the right of a burn. The path climbs more steps and then descends another flight of steps, swinging right to reach the River Tweed.

► From here a lovely riverbank path leads to a long flight of steps, which swing right to a gate. Go through the gate, cross a short strip of grassland and then turn left onto a pavement. At the next junction turn right onto Pinnaclehill Park, then take the first left to reach the B6350.

► Turn left and follow the pavement as it drops gently back down towards the River Tweed. Just before reaching Hunter's Bridge turn right onto a cycletrack, which climbs gradually and bears right onto the A698. Turn left and walk across Hunter's Bridge back over the Tweed – there are fine views along the river from the bridge. Once across the bridge, and before reaching a roundabout, turn left down a flight of steps and then left again onto Mayfield Riverside Walk.

Trading Place Sir Walter Scott called Kelso 'the most beautiful if not the most romantic village in Scotland'. Its name translates from Old English *Calc How* as 'Place of the Chalk Hill'. It has been spelt in different ways over the years, including Calkou and Kelcou. It has stood at the confluence of the River Tweed and River Teviot since 1128 when Kelso Abbey was founded. Some of the street names around the town provide evidence of Kelso's history as a market town; Woolmarket, Coalmarket, Mill Wynd and Distillery Lane offer clues to the trades that built the town.

Almost as well known as Kelso Abbey is Floors Castle, the seat of the Duke of Roxburgh, which stands on the outskirts of the town and is the largest inhabited house in Scotland. William Adam designed much of Floors Castle in 1721 (Adam also designed Hopetoun House in South Queensferry and Pollok House in Glasgow); William Playfair, Scotland's leading architect of the time, added to it in 1837.

► This single-track road swings right and makes its way through a lovely strip of parkland, again along the banks of the River Tweed, where heron, swans and mallard can be seen. The riverside walk passes several houses, continuing all the way through the park and returning to Rennie's Bridge.

► Bear right up a slope back to Bridge Street. Turn right and follow Bridge Street back to The Square.

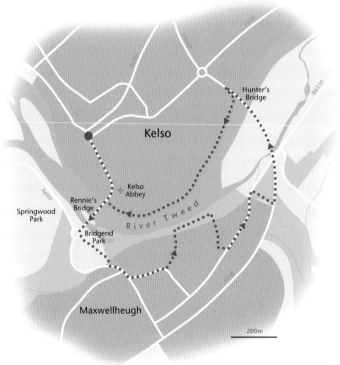

Kelso from Bridgend Park

River Tweed near Norham

Norham and Norham Castle

Distance 5.75km/3.5 miles
Time 1 hour 45
Start/Finish Village Green, Norham
GR NT899473
Terrain Woodland, field edge and
riverbank paths, quiet roads and
pavement
Map OS Landranger 74
Public transport Perryman's Bus
Service 67 between Galashiels and
Berwick-upon-Tweed to Norham

After Coldstream, the River Tweed
divides Scotland from England
until it passes the little village of
Horncliffe, where it leaves Scotland
behind to enter Northumberland.
Norham is the first village on the
English side of the border that
the Tweed makes contact with.
An excellent walk leaves from
Norham, with a mixture of lovely
riverbank and woodland paths
and a quiet section of road
arriving at the historic remains
of Norham Castle.

► From Norham Village Green walk
down Pedwell Way to St Cuthbert's
Church. Go through the gates into the
church grounds and turn left, then
immediately right onto a grassy track,
which makes its way to the right of the
church through the graveyard. This
leads to a narrow path, which continues
down to the Tweed.

► Drop down a flight of steps to a
broad path, turn left and follow this west
alongside a lovely section of the river,
which is very popular with anglers. As
the path approaches the four-arched
Ladykirk and Norham Bridge, bear right
onto a path, walk under the bridge and
then swing left to a stile.

► Go over the stile, turn right and follow
a field-edge path south towards a
scattering of houses on the outskirts of
Norham. Just before reaching a house
turn right over a stile, then left to follow a
woodland path which passes through a
gate to gain a narrow road. Turn right
and follow this to its end. Take a gate on
the right signposted for 'Twizell Bridge'
with a grassy path now proceeding
alongside the Tweed. This travels by a
couple of attractive cottages and through
another gate where a narrower,
undulating path continues along a
stunning section of the Tweed. Once

Both Sides of the Border Straddling
the River Tweed and the Scottish/English
Border, the Ladykirk and Norham Bridge
was built between 1885 and 1887 to
replace an earlier wooden bridge,
which had been erected in 1838. As it
extends into both England and Scotland,
English Heritage has listed the Ladykirk
and Norham Bridge as a Grade II
structure, while Historic Scotland make
it a category B.

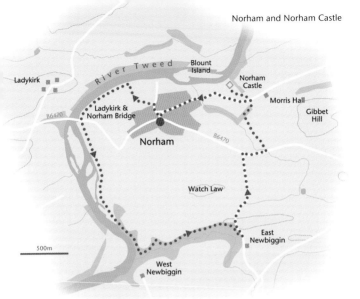

through another gate, go left at a junction (an old footbridge is to the right) and through some thicker woodland. At the next fork go left up a steep flight of steps, then through some scrubby woodland to a junction.

► Go right and follow this path under an impressive old railway arch into Newbiggin Wood. The path continues easily (although a little muddy at times) and crosses a stile. Bear right at a fork, signposted 'East Newbiggin', to follow the grassy path through some beautiful countryside to a gate. Go through here, then turn left onto a quiet road which wends its way through peaceful countryside, passing by what used to

be Norham Station (now converted into houses) to reach the B6470, a little east of Norham.

► Turn right onto the B6470 and, soon after, turn left onto a path signposted for Norham Castle. Cross a footbridge and then go through a gate into a field. Walk straight on along the field edge and pass through a gate onto a woodland path. Follow this until it reaches a footbridge on the left. Go over this and through a gate, and then turn right and follow a field edge through another gate to a road beside Norham Castle. Turn left and walk the short distance along the road to the entrance to the castle.

► Retrace your steps to the road, turn right and drop down along the pavement into Norham, following Castle Street back to the village green.

Dangerous Liaison Ranulf Flambard, the Bishop of Durham, founded Norham Castle in 1121. Between 1136 and 1513 it fell into Scottish hands four times. There were another five unsuccessful attempts, on one occasion by Robert the Bruce, and this saw Norham Castle gain the reputation as the most dangerous place in England.

The last attempt by the Scots came only a few weeks after the catastrophic Battle of Flodden, when 10,000 men, including King James IV, were killed. Because of the ongoing attacks, Norham Castle spent much of its life undergoing repairs; considerable damage was caused by the infamous Mons Meg, which is now on display at Edinburgh Castle. Its time as an important stronghold came to an end in 1559, when Queen Elizabeth I took control from the Bishop of Durham, Cuthbert Tunstall, after he refused to swear an Oath of Supremacy to the Queen. Norham Castle quickly fell into disrepair.

Celebrated artist J M W Turner visited and sketched Norham Castle in 1797 and produced a series of vibrant watercolours depicting a bustling River Tweed and Norham Castle at sunrise.

Ladykirk and Norham Bridge

Norham Castle

The inscription on the monument reads:

SIR ALEC DOUGLAS-HOME KT PC KT
STATESMAN AND COUNTRYMAN
14 EARL OF HOME
LORD HOME OF THE HIRSEL
PRIME MINISTER FOREIGN SECRETARY

UNVEILED BY
HRH PRINCE OF WALES
23RD AUGUST

THE GENEROSITY OF
HIS FELLOW BORDERERS
MADE THIS MONUMENT
POSSIBLE

1903
1995

Statue of Sir Alec Douglas-Home

Hirsel Country Park

Distance 7.75km/4.75 miles
Time 2 hours 30
Start/Finish Hirsel Country Park car
park, Coldstream GR NT827402
Terrain Woodland paths and tracks,
estate roads, steep slopes
Map OS Landranger 74
Public transport Perryman's Bus
Service 67 between Berwick-upon-
Tweed and Coldstream to Hirsel
Estate entrance

**This woodland walk explores the
lovely surroundings of Hirsel
Country Park which lies at the
western edge of Coldstream.
The estate has been under the
stewardship of the Home
(pronounced Hume) family since
the early 17th century. The trees
are host to a variety of wildlife
and Hirsel Lake is a wildfowl
sanctuary. The walk mostly follows
waymarks; one section does make its
way above steep slopes, although
this can be easily avoided.**

► From the car park turn left by
the tearoom at a yellow and red
waymark. Walk by the tearoom and
other estate buildings onto a grassy
track between the golf course and
woodland. Pass a path on the right,
then bear right onto a narrow
woodland path which continues
alongside the golf course. Once across

a footbridge walk through the wood,
soon crossing the Leet Water by another
bridge and then passing through a gate
onto the golf course. Bear left onto a
path, then at the next fork head right
from the golf course through another
gate back into woodland.

► With the Leet Water below to the
left, follow the path north. The trees are
ablaze with colour during the autumn
whilst the woodland floor is scattered
with wildflowers during the spring and
summer. At a fork go left, then bear left
onto another path. Easy progress is
made to the next fork where the yellow
waymarks are left behind.

Yes, Prime Minister A monument to
Sir Alec Douglas-Home stands at the
entrance gate of Hirsel Country Park.
Born in London in 1903, Douglas-Home
became the 14th Earl of Hirsel in 1951
upon the death of his father, but had to
relinquish the title in 1963 and give up
his seat in the House of Lords when he
succeeded Harold Macmillan as Prime
Minister. The Conservative Party had lost
standing following the Profuma scandal,
however, and his tenure lasted less than
a year. He later took charge of Foreign
and Commonwealth Affairs in the Heath
government of the 1970s. Sir Alec
Douglas-Home died at Hirsel in 1995
and is buried at Lennel Cemetery on the
outskirts of Coldstream.

► Go right, now following red waymarks and continuing along the left edge of the wood with the impressive Hirsel House sitting away to the left. The path is largely well maintained, although it can be muddy at times. It eventually comes to a track. For the optional shorter route avoiding the section of path along steeper slopes, turn left onto the track and cross the Dunglass Bridge over the Leet Water before veering left onto a red waymarked path (jump forward three paragraphs for subsequent directions).

► To continue the longer walk go straight across the track onto a narrow path, which makes its way northwest above the Leet with steep slopes dropping down to the left. In due course an impressive monument is reached at a clearing. Alexander, Earl of Home, erected the monument for his son William, Lord Dunglas, who was killed at the age of 25 in the Battle of Guildford in America.

► Continue by the monument back into woodland. At a junction, turn left, then immediately right onto a yellow waymarked path which then crosses the Leet Water via a wooden bridge. Go through a gate and then turn right to follow the path as it climbs a slope to a broad estate track. Turn left and follow this peaceful track southeast through some lovely countryside, alongside woodland, eventually dropping down to a crossroads. Turn left towards the Dunglass Bridge, but just before you reach it turn right onto a path at a red marker – this is where the shorter route is picked up.

► Follow this wooded path, turning right at a fork and then left onto a broad track which passes the famous Hirsel Highland cattle and a large red sandstone house. An estate road swings right by the Cow Arch and then past the house.

► At a three-way junction go right (now following yellow waymarks) and

Home Land King James IV granted the 3000-acre Hirsel Estate lands to the Douglas-Home family in 1621. Part of Hirsel House was built around this time, and many of the trees were planted on the estate. Hirsel Estate has always been famous for its salmon fishing, and it was on the River Tweed that the 8th Earl of Home caught an enormous 69-pound salmon in 1743. In 1786 Hirsel Lake was created, and today seasonal wildlife on the lake includes heron, little grebe, moorhen, mute and whooper swans, pochard, shoveler, tufted duck, goosander, water rails, reed bunting and sedge warbler.

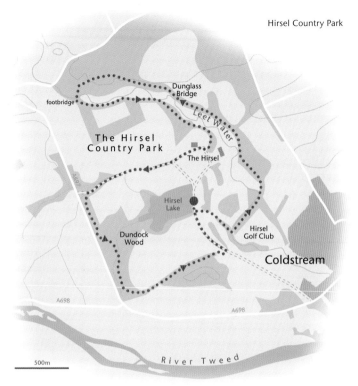

walk along the estate road through pleasant countryside. At a fork keep straight on and follow the road until just short of the A697. Turn left onto a waymarked path into Dundock Wood and follow this as it winds through the woodland, soon swinging left. Turn right at the next waymark where the path, which can be a little overgrown, passes over a section of boardwalk. Go left at the next junction,

then right at the next. Another right turn gains a broad muddy track which meanders its way through beech woodland for some time, granting fine rural views.

► Eventually the track drops down to a cottage. Skirt to the right around this and left by a second cottage to return to the estate road. Turn left and follow this back to the start.

145

Leet Water bridge in Hirsel Country Park

Coldstream

Coldstream

Distance 5.75km/3.5 miles
Time 2 hours
Start/Finish Henderson Park, Coldstream GR NT844399
Terrain Pavement, woodland and riverside paths
Map OS Landranger 74
Public transport Perryman's Bus Service 67 between Berwick-upon-Tweed and Coldstream

The Scottish Borders come to an end and Northumberland begins at the centre of the River Tweed at Coldstream. The magnificent Coldstream Bridge spans both countries. This pleasing walk sticks to the Scottish side of the River Tweed and circles around Coldstream, chiefly by way of riverbank and woodland paths.

▶ From Henderson Park, which gives good views of the Tweed (there is a small car park here as well), turn left and walk along High Street through the town. Just before a roadbridge over the Leet Water, walk down a flight of steps and turn left onto a path which runs alongside the Leet Water. Cross over a road onto Penitents Walk, following the path between the river and a wall to reach a gate on the right.

▶ Go through here onto a track which runs towards the Tweed. It soon ends,

but keep heading over parkland to the riverbank, turn left and walk above the banks of the Tweed and up a flight of steps. Turn right onto Nun's Walk, which climbs gradually above the Tweed, passing the 70ft-high monument to

....

Guards of Honour Coldstream identifies itself as 'the First True Border Toon'. It was destroyed twice by the army of Edward I during the Border Wars, and again 250 years later by the army of Henry VIII. It says much about the tenacity of the townsfolk that Coldstream exists at all.

Both Scottish and English armies have crossed the River Tweed at Coldstream en route to various battles, most famously when King James IV marched his Scottish army a few miles southeast to fight the Earl of Surrey's English Army on Flodden Field in 1513. The battle was a catastrophe for the Scots: up to 10,000 men were killed, the King and many members of the nobility amongst them.

Coldstream has become best known as the home of the Coldstream Guards. Formed in 1650, they were originally known as Monck's Regiment on Foot, named after General Monck, Oliver Cromwell's military governor in Scotland. In 1670 the name changed to the Coldstream Guards, and it is the oldest regiment in the regular army in continuous active service. The excellent Coldstream Museum details all there is to know about this historic regiment.

Charles Albany Marjoribanks, an MP for Berwickshire between 1832 and his death at the age of 39 in 1833.

▶ Turn right onto the A698 and follow the pavement down towards Coldstream Bridge. Just before the bridge and the Toll House – which, during the 18th century, rivalled Gretna Green as the place for 'runaway' weddings – turn right, descending a flight of steps and then going left to walk underneath Coldstream Bridge.

▶ A path then leads past the Cauld Weir and over a footbridge before passing an impressive fisherman's hut. It turns left through a gate, then right through the next gate onto a wide grassy path – continue northeast for approximately 0.75 miles between a fenced field and the River Tweed to reach the edge of a wood near Lennel.

▶ At this point turn left, pass through two gates and then turn left through another gate where a path swings right and travels southwest parallel to the Tweed – this section can be a little overgrown. Walk along the fenced path through two gates and then on another fenced path to a flight of stone steps and a ramp. Take either to gain a woodland path and then turn left. This attractive path runs above fields to a fork. Take the left branch, keeping straight ahead, and continue past a gate to where the path splits.

▶ Take the left fork to continue through woodland by a path alongside a burn. Just before the A6112, the path turns left over the burn and continues to a gate. Go through the gate, cross a minor road and, beyond another gate, turn right at a fork. Continue for a few metres to reach the A6112.

▶ Go straight across this onto another beautiful woodland path. This carries on through a strip of woodland along the outskirts of Coldstream for around one third of a mile to meet a field-edge path. Turn left to follow the path by some

Burns' Border Bridge The eye-catching seven-arched Coldstream Bridge was constructed between 1763 and 1767 at a cost of £6000. The prolific civil engineer, John Smeaton, designed it: Perth Bridge, and a section of the Forth & Clyde Canal are other examples of Smeaton's work. The bridge replaced an old ford that had connected Scotland with England for many years. Robert Burns crossed Coldstream Bridge into England for the first time in his life when touring the Borders in May 1787. His companion and fellow writer Robert Ainslie claimed that on reaching the English side, Burns took off his hat, knelt down and delivered several lines from his classic poem, 'The Cotter's Saturday Night', in reverence to his beloved Scotland.

houses onto a road. Continue straight on to a fork. Take the right branch and then turn right onto Duns Road. A first left leads onto Bennecourt Drive.

► Follow the pavement as it drops gently down to North Mews. Go left onto North Mews, then left again to reach a junction. Turn right onto a woodland path and after just a few metres go left at a crossroads. Keep with the path to pass some playing fields and, once through a gate, turn left, then right and walk through Home Park car park onto the High Street. Turn left and walk back to Henderson Park.

Coldstream Bridge

Tweed Estuary

Berwick-upon-Tweed and the Tweed Estuary

Distance 9.25km/5.75 miles
Time 2 hours 30
Start/Finish Berwick Town Hall, Berwick-upon-Tweed GR NT998529
Terrain Pavement, woodland and riverside paths
Map OS Landranger 75
Public transport Cross Country Railways and Perryman's Bus Service 253 between Edinburgh and Berwick-upon-Tweed. East Coast Railways and Arriva Northumbria Coach Service 505 between Newcastle and Berwick-upon-Tweed

The River Tweed has a fitting finale at the historic town of Berwick-upon-Tweed. This walk encompasses much of what the town is famous for, including its celebrated walls and the three bridges that span the river. The route also travels along the Tweed Estuary, famed for its wildlife. Lovely countryside views provide a pleasant contrast to Berwick-upon-Tweed's compact streets.

▶ From the striking Town Hall, walk along Marygate, passing Golden Square. Just before the Elizabethan Scots Gate archway turn left and climb a narrow road. At the top of the slope take a sharp right through a gate onto the town walls. Cross Scots Gate onto a path and

by the Cumberland Bastion to a fork beside the Brass Bastion. Bear right here and continue along the top of the wall by the impressive Berwick Barracks. Built in 1717 they are one of the oldest purpose-built barracks in Britain and were home to the King's Own Scottish Borderers – the barracks are now a museum.

Border Control From the early 11th century Berwick-upon-Tweed was one of Scotland's main ports, and this remained the case until Edward I sacked the town in 1296. By 1482, Berwick had changed hands no fewer than 14 times due to its position at the outflow of the River Tweed, seen by many as the border between Scotland and England.

The remains of Berwick Castle and the magnificent walls and bastions that surround the town offer tangible evidence of what was required to defend Berwick from many different armies. The ties with Scotland are not completely severed, however, as the local football team, Berwick Rangers, play in the Scottish League.

Berwick town centre is dominated by its Town Hall and this, as well as the tight streets and lanes, inspired the artist L S Lowry (1887-1976) throughout his many visits to the town from the 1930s until his death.

▶ Keep to the path as it continues south and beyond a gate walk by Fisher's Fort and then Coxon's Tower. The path sweeps right and travels above the River Tweed to Bridge End.

▶ Go straight on past Berwick Bridge onto a narrow cobble-stoned road and at its end turn left to a fork. Go left underneath the Royal Tweed Bridge where the path drops down to the Tweed, soon passing under the Royal Border Bridge and then an archway of Berwick Castle. The path now heads west along the Tweed Estuary, which is popular with anglers and wildlife – swans, heron, roe deer, badger and otter are a small selection of the creatures that may be spotted amongst the fine rural scenery.

....

Triumphal Archways The famous old Berwick Bridge took fifteen years to build, eventually opening in 1626. It is a Grade 1 listed stone bridge. Slightly further upstream is the 1405ft-long Royal Tweed Bridge, which opened in 1928. However, it is the exceptional 28-arch Royal Border Bridge, designed by the civil engineer Robert Stephenson, which dominates. This wonderful viaduct was the final link of the Newcastle to Berwick railway line, and was opened in 1850 by Queen Victoria. The bridge is over 2000ft in length and rises to 125ft above the river.

▶ Once by the second of two cottages the path enters some dense woodland. This can be muddy at times as it continues for approximately half a mile to gain a path on the left, signposted 'Berwick By-Pass Bridge'. Follow this down through a gate, emerging from the woodland beside the Tweed.

▶ Go over the footbridge and then bear right to cross a field towards an old ruined building. Just before the ruin turn left onto a path which runs along a low embankment to the left of a hedge. The path soon peters out, but continue alongside the hedge towards the by-pass bridge. Once over a stile a slightly overgrown path continues over a second stile where the path now climbs up to the Berwick By-Pass Bridge and the A1.

▶ Turn left to follow the pavement over the River Tweed. Soon after the bridge, turn left over a stile onto a public footpath signposted for Berwick. Walk through a car park, then swing left onto a path crossing a picnic area. Turn right onto a waymarked path which drops down through woodland and over a bridge. After rising gently above the river a lovely field-edge path then continues northeast, leading to a single-track road. Turn left, and, as the road swings right, go through a wooden gate on the left. Follow a path as it turns left, skirting woodland, to another gate.

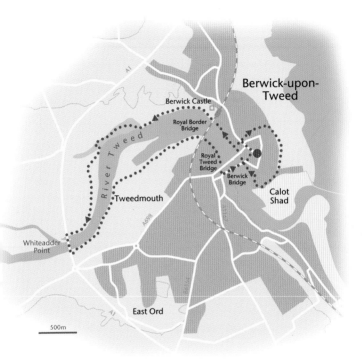

The path, which is overgrown at times, proceeds by a water treatment facility and the floodplains of Yarrow Slake.

▶ After you have passed through three gates in quick succession a better path approaches Berwick, eventually swinging right and then left into a field. Take the left fork, cross the field and just before the Royal Border Bridge go left through a gate onto a track which passes under the bridge and onto Riverside Road. Turn left and then, after a small car park, go left again and follow the path on under the Royal Tweed Bridge. Turn left onto Berwick Bridge to cross back over the River Tweed onto Bridge End. Cross Bridge Street onto West Street, which climbs steeply back to Marygate and the Town Hall.

Royal Border Bridge

Index